"Our experiences have taught us that leaders are far better off when they devise structures, procedures and processes in collaboration with the people who have to make them work. This increases the breadth of ideas and builds a broader base of ownership. It creates both the freedoms and the fences that are necessary for flexibility and creativity. In many cases, the inmates are the only resource that can save the asylum."

~ Lee Ozley and Rich Teerlink, *More than a Motorcycle, The Harley-Davidson Story*

Table of Contents

Foreword

The data on employee engagement inside organizations in the U.S. is far from stellar. In 2008 some studies had the number of employees who feel *disengaged* in the 20-25% range and another 30% on average feel only *somewhat engaged*. While there are exceptions to the rule, Southwest Airlines, Whole Foods, W.L. Gore and Associates, most U.S. organizations still fall woefully short of engaging their people as fully as they could. While most leaders would agree with the statement that "the people closest to the work know best how to improve it", it seems policies, practices, ingrained habits and thinking seem to stifle any significant movement toward truly acting on that belief.

There are three trends that point to a possible change in this pattern and that may lead toward more engagement between "management" and "employees." The first is that our systems are becoming more interconnected and complex. From our Systems Thinking and Complexity Science fields, we know that as systems become more diverse and interconnected (i.e. interdependent), they become less predictable and more immune to top-down plans and actions. As an example, who can know when the next incident of a raw material being manufactured in some remote region of the world when added to something else in another part of the world, causes a calamity? The complexity of our evolving systems means that no one person or "expert" can know the right course of action or make any guarantees of continuous predictable outcomes. We must be willing to assemble and engage all stakeholders, *especially those closest to the action*, in an ongoing dialogue if we're going to find a *sustainable* response to these complex and often unpredictable challenges as they arise.

The second trend is that employees across the globe are more educated and getting smarter and more sophisticated, not less. This means they come into the workplace with *higher* expectations for involvement in decision-making, and if they are not given wide latitude in how they do their work, they have no compunction about going somewhere where they do. And with so much information work able to be done from home, people are choosing to be free agents over working in authoritarian organizations.

The last trend is the ever-growing influence of the Internet and the speed and availability of information that can be put into employee hands. With technology advances like cloud computing, with just a mobile device, employees can access information just about anywhere. This means they can act on it immediately rather than waiting for commands to come down from management.

Going down the path of fuller engagement is not for the faint of heart. The transparency and amount of letting go required of management can be quite scary. From the employee side of things, this means they have to acknowledge they can no longer remain "innocent". By innocent I mean they can no longer pretend that the gnarly challenges facing any business that wants to grow and sustain itself are "management's job". They must also be ready to face the consequences of their increased involvement in decision-making. No more, "I just did what my manager told me" excuses. Make no mistake, for every manager who is scared of letting go and turning over the "how", there is a corresponding employee who is ambivalent about being more accountable for the whole. This is what Peter Block means when he says that the greatest act of love a manager can show an employee is to "confront them with their freedom."

Yet, I still believe that the majority of employees will step up to the challenge when given the chance and I have seen it first hand in working with employee teams over the years. More often, they are hungry to be challenged more and *want* to help improve the whole. The challenge typically is to get management to open up the books and decision-making to more people. This might scare some of those in management, but the upside is huge. The message for organizations is pretty clear, figure out ways to involve and engage people more fully and effectively or be left behind by those organizations that do.

Because storytelling is such an effective and familiar communication tool, I've chosen to tell a story of what *could be* in relation to how we engage the people inside our organizations more deeply and meaningfully.

Rich McLaughlin, July 2009

The Players

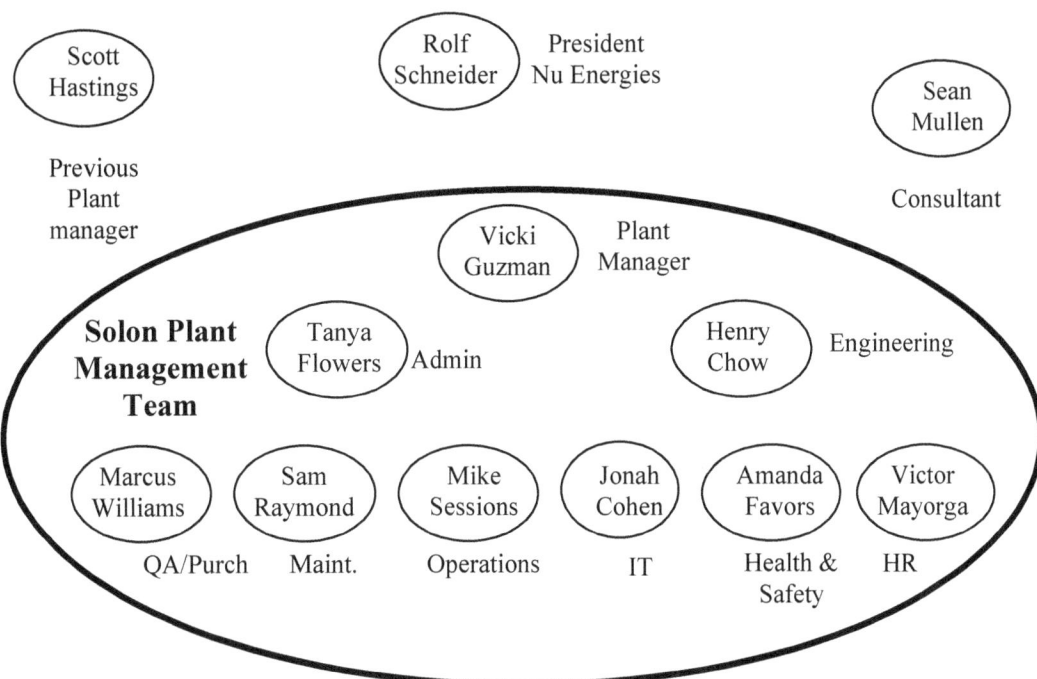

Scott Hastings
Previous Plant manager

Rolf Schneider — President Nu Energies

Sean Mullen — Consultant

Solon Plant Management Team

Vicki Guzman — Plant Manager

Tanya Flowers — Admin

Henry Chow — Engineering

Marcus Williams — QA/Purch

Sam Raymond — Maint.

Mike Sessions — Operations

Jonah Cohen — IT

Amanda Favors — Health & Safety

Victor Mayorga — HR

Supervisors: Ryan Sacco, Hector Maldanado, Kisha Wells, Vijay Patel

Line Employees: ~90 including: Lisa Williams, Steve, Michael, Trish, Ving, Myla and Ty

Solon Corporate Office: Ryan Connclly — Sales/Marketing

Integrators (customers)

- Solar Solutions
- Sun Works
- Solar Consulting
- New Energy Options

Solon Corporation - Background

Solon Corporation was one of the later entrants into the solar energy market. Started by two entrepreneurs in the San Francisco area in the early 90's, Solon initially focused on a grass-roots approach to growing their market by making home conversion kits for single homeowners who wanted to explore installing solar panels. As the business grew they saw that the commercial market offered better scalability and margins, but they still liked serving the individual homeowners. Currently 80% of their product is sold to various "Integrators" who serve a retail function and install the panels for the end customer.

By 2000 Solon had grown enough that it was more than the founders could handle and they sold the business to Nu Energies, Ltd., a holding company with many promising start-ups serving niches in the alternative energy arena. In early 2008, sensing an increased appetite for solar options, Solon expanded faster than the market was ready to absorb and ended up with some excess capacity in product and people. Nu Energies management told the plant manager, Scott Hastings, to let about 20% of their workforce go leaving about 120 people at the plant. Scott did not handle the ramp up in a sustainable fashion and was less than diplomatic and objective around whom to layoff. Soon after, he was let go, and Henry Chow, Engineering Manager was made acting plant manager. Nu Energies then decided to bring in an outsider to re-engage people at the plant.

Friday afternoon 3:15, March 9

47 year-old Vicki Guzman is sitting in the office of Rolf Schneider, President of Nu Energies in Los Angeles. Rolf has brought Vicki in to recharge efforts at Solon's single manufacturing facility in Hayward, California. Rolf knows Vicki from their time working together at Bryson Energy and knows she is up for the task.

Rolf leaning back in his chair, "What's the hesitancy all about Vicki? I know you can do this."

"I just want to make sure you know what we're in for, Rolf." Vicki replies "The good news is that demand is still high for solar options so I don't think we have to worry there, but as you know, you tried to push solar product out there before the infrastructure was in place and you ended up with excess capacity both in product and people. Now it looks like you've made the right corrections. What I need to know now is whether you're going to be OK with only 2-4% growth for the next 3 years because that's what its going to be if you ultimately want to get back on a path of *sustainable* growth. That *is* what you want, correct?" Vicki eyes him carefully.

Rolf steeples his hands and looks off in contemplation for a moment. Vicki waits him out. He finally leans forward putting his hands on his desk, "Yes, yes, of course, but what *I* want to know is what can you guarantee me if I give you that time?"

"Given current favorable political winds, we can probably put ourselves in a position to grow in the 6-8% range for at least 5 years and possibly 10 assuming we can get a robust process going in the Hayward facility and we then set up another on the east coast. Beyond that I think we'd be guessing." Vicki replies.

Rolf interrupts, "I thought you said 8-12%!?!"

Vicki counters, "No Rolf, *you* said that. I said it's possible, but I won't know for sure until I get in there and start things going and see how things are. Besides, you know the economy is still recovering. And that leads to the other thing I need you to understand, it's what I call remembering to 'go slow to go fast'. I spent all last week talking to people from all parts of the plant, and you need to know some are still hurt, confused, scared and wondering if they're next."

"But we've told them multiple times, that we don't anticipate any layoffs for the near future!" Rolf said, exasperated.

"Yes, but the layoffs are still fresh in their mind, and as we've discussed Hastings could have done a much better job of handling that!" Vicki points out.

Rolf leans forward holding up his hands "I know, I know, let's not go there again."

"OK, but if this is the first real layoffs the company has had, it's going to take some time to win back their full trust. Plus, I'm the new gal in town!" Vicki replies.

"So, what's your plan to win them over?" Rolf leans back again.

"Well, I still don't have a good feel for how things really run yet. When I was visiting with plant people this week, I know people were trying to put their best foot forward and shine me on a bit. I'd like to spend my first month just getting a *real* hands-on feel for the business, the operations and the people." Vicki says.

"I don't think you're team is going to like you digging into their areas, especially, Henry." Reminded Rolf.

"I think I can do it without seeming overbearing." Vicki responds. "With Henry, I plan on appealing to his ego and ask him to basically oversee production until I've had a chance to look around."

"That sounds risk-eee" Rolf singsongs.

"Maybe" Vicki replies, "but I've pushed my agenda to quickly too many times before to fall into that trap again."

The Management Team

Monday morning, March 12, 7:15 a.m.

Vicki is at her desk preparing for her first meeting with the entire management team and is thinking about the group she has inherited. From her conversations with Rolf and Scott Hastings, plus her observations meeting with each of the plant management team one-on-one, and from roaming the plant last week, she has learned the following:

Henry Chow – Manager of Engineering, 41 years old, husband and father of one boy. Henry has an electrical engineering background and has been a solid, steady manager in his 5 years at Solon. He was seen as next in line to become plant manager and was not happy about hearing of an outsider being brought in. In his first meeting with Vicki he was cool, but polite. Henry is known as being very bright, but a little reserved in his ways with others and is working on being more approachable and assertive. He knows the industry and the product nuances better than anyone at the plant. He is well regarded by his peers and deferential to upper management.

Amanda Favors – Manager of Health and Safety, Amanda, 34, married 4 years and no kids. She was hired right out of college into Solon as a production supervisor and worked her way over to health and safety. She is seen as quiet, but passionate about safety and proud of the safety record under her tenure. She can get a little rigid in her zeal for safety but is seen as someone who's heart is in the right place. She seemed a little nervous and distracted in her first meeting with Vicki.

Jonah Cohen - Manager IT, Jonah, 31 and single, is the resident comedian. He has a quirky sense of humor that allows him to bring up touchy subjects in a way that disarms people. He is an IT whiz, but sometimes seems more interested in his music and his latest Crowdsourcing idea than anything else. When the team can keep him focused, he often is able to come up with some very unique ideas, but tends to lose interest during implementation phase.

Marcus Williams, Quality Manager, Marcus, a 38 year old divorced father of two, Marcus has been at Solon for 11 years. He is very knowledgeable about quality systems but can be a bit strident and arrogant on occasion. The rest of the team respect his knowledge, but wish he would get off his Quality soapbox and remember that we're trying to run a profitable business. Because the quality of incoming raw material is so critical to operations, Marcus oversees the Purchasing function for the plant as well.

Victor Mayorga, Human Resources Manager, Victor is a 54 year old father of 3 girls and has been at Solon since its inception. Victor prides himself on having a good relationship with rank and file employees, but does not see the downside to the "kindly father" approach he takes when dealing with them. He is not a rock the boat type and would like to quietly close out his time at Solon over the next 5 years. The layoffs were particularly hard for him because it was the first time it has happened at Solon.

Mike Sessions, Operations Manager. A 35 year old, divorced father of two girls, Mike was hired by Scott, the previous plant manager and has been in charge of daily operations for the past 3 years. He reports to Henry, but Henry pretty much leaves him alone as long as productivity numbers are good. Mike was not happy about Scott being let go and feels a bit under the gun. His people, especially his 4 supervisors, have noticed he is much more abrupt these days and more demanding. One of Solon's better supervisors just left for another position 3 weeks ago, and Henry was concerned, but Mike reassured him that it was for a better position and that he had things "under control."

Sam Raymond, Maintenance Manager, Sam is a 57 year-old married father of 3 who came from the microchip industry and has extensive experience with clean rooms. He has been at Solon 2 years and likes the idea of ending his time with a solar energy company as it reminds him of his hippie college days at Cal. He keeps to himself, but is seen as someone whose knowledge extends beyond the maintenance area. Vicki came away from her meeting with him sensing that while he seems very knowledgeable and worldly, he seems content to just run on cruise control and keep a low profile.

Tanya Flowers, Administrative Assistant, Tanya is a 28 year-old single mom of one boy. She was Scott's assistant for 3 years and now supports Vicki and the rest of the team. She is a hardworking and conscientious, but tends to keep to herself. Previously, Scott did not have her sit in on the team meetings, but Vicki told her that she should. Tanya was surprised, but happy to be more involved.

Part 1:

A Call to a Higher Standard

"Most leaders think too small, and as a result, they do not capture the imaginations of the deep-rooted commitment of their people. At the same time, by choosing a modest path, they encounter a horde of other marginal leaders who do not possess the inner strength to pursue great visions. Instead of blazing new, exciting, and rewarding trails, they join the pack of mediocre leaders and accept modest results. That is unfortunate indeed, because they deny us all a better life in the process."

~ Neil Snyder, et al. *Vision, Values, Courage: Leadership for Quality Management*

Monday, March 12, 8:05 a.m.

The plant management team is gathered around a conference table in the main conference room. When Vicki comes in, she purposely chooses to sit at the head position. Normally she avoids this type of thing preferring to downplay her authority, but today she wants it clear who is in charge, especially after what she plans to tell them.

"OK let's get started!" Vicki waits while people get settled in their seats. "I've met with each of you individually, but this is our first time together as a group and I appreciate everyone making the effort to be on time." Vicki pauses. "Now, a few things before we get into any nitty gritty daily production discussion. I want to give you a few thoughts as to my understanding of where we are and what's ahead of us." Vicki pauses again to make eye contact with everyone around the table, "This company makes good product and is respected in the field. If anything, our only sin was trying to grow faster than the marketplace could support. Now, we've had to do some regrouping, but I think we're poised well to go forward. Sales continue to be solid, but we are having some problems reining in costs and some quality issues have surfaced."

Marcus looks to speak up, but Vicki waves him off. "I'm not trying to assign blame here Marcus, just stating the facts."

To the group…"How am I doing so far?" Vicki asks.

"I think you nailed it boss" Mike says enthusiastically. Jonah rolls his eyes at Mike's attempt to suckup.

"Thanks Mike, but *please*..everyone…call me *Vicki*" Vicki replies.

She continues, "Now a couple things about what my immediate plans are. First, I'm guessing you probably have a lot of questions about me and for me and are wondering when is the right time to bring them up. I can tell you that it *won't* be today, but I'd like us to block out 3 hours next week to go through what's called a Leadership Assimilation. It's something I've gone through before in another leadership role and I found it a nice way to accelerate relationships and candor in the team. Basically, it's a process where you get to tee up whatever question you want to ask while I'm out of the room and I come back in and try my best to answer them. A friend of mine who is a management consultant and coach will take us through the process. Tanya will work with all of you to find a three hour block that works for everybody. It may be that we just extend our weekly team meeting next Monday the 3 extra hours, but again, I'll let Tanya work that out with you."

Vicki pauses, "Now, the second and really last item for me today. I still don't have an in-depth feel for Solon's customers yet, so I've been in touch with Ryan Connelly out of the Sales office and he has me set up with a week of ride-alongs with some Sales and Marketing people."

Everyone sits up a little straighter at this news and eyebrows raise. Vicki noticing this said, "Yes, that means I will be out *all* week. You did fine with Henry acting as plant manager for the last 3 months, so I figure another week should not be an issue. Henry, are you OK with that?"

Henry sits up even straighter, blinks and looks around the room, saying "Sure I guess so."

Noticing his hesitance Vicki asked, "Is there a concern?"

"No, I guess I'm just wondering how you want to be kept informed." He replied.

"Let's plan on touching base on the phone the beginning and end of each day for now." Vicki replies. Moving her gaze around the room, she continues "and I will certainly be accessible throughout each day, so don't hesitate to call or e-mail me. If it's just an update or FYI type of thing, send me an e-mail. If you need me to get back to you that day, better to call me." Vicki replies firmly.

"Any other questions?" Vicki looks around the table.

Marcus chimes in, "There are some product quality issues we were going to discuss this morning."

Victor adds, "And we were going to discuss who should fill a supervisor position."

Everyone looks at Vicki expectantly.

"Use your best judgment and carry on as you have." She replies amiably. "Again, you can reach me by phone if you feel you need my input….sound good?"

Vicki gathers her stuff up and as she exits announces, "You may see me popping in and out of my office during the week to get this or that, but pretty much consider me out for the week." Looking directly at Henry, "Henry, It's all yours. I'll call you at the end of the day."

Initially everyone is quiet after she leaves. Henry is puzzled. *What was that all about he wonders.*

"Well, …that was interesting" laughs Jonah.

"What's your take on that Henry?" Mike asks.

Henry continues to look down thinking, then looks up at Mike. "I honestly don't know, but we got stuff to go over so I guess we should get at it." He picks up his copy of the weekly production report and says "Okay, item 1…"

Monday, March 12, 9:35 a.m.

The meeting has broken up and Mike catches up with Henry and together they walk down the hallway toward the cafeteria. "So what was up with that little bomb she set off about being out all week? Not exactly a strong leadership statement for you first full week at work, huh?" Mike asks wanting to feel Henry out.

"I don't know.." Henry muses "I wish I had done the same when I started – a week to just go around with Sales and meet customers directly – would have been extremely valuable now that I think about it."

Mike is undeterred, "Yeah, but it almost seems like she's testing you, man. With her *'Henry it's all yours'*."

Henry growing a little leary of where Mike's trying to go with this, "Yeah, maybe, but if I had to choose between someone looking over my shoulder vs. leaving me alone, I'll take the latter any day." Henry speeds up his walk, "Look I have a call I need to make, I'll see you later."

Mike stops in his tracks and looks a little disappointed as he watches Henry continue down the hallway.

Tuesday March 13, 1:15

Marcus is finishing up his lunch in the cafeteria when Jonah joins him.

"Hey Marcus, you got a minute?" Jonah asks, "I want to talk to you about that social networking software I want to tryout."

"What's it going to cost?" Marcus eyes him warily.

"Nothing right now, I spoke to the makers and they agreed to let us try it out for 6 months as long as we keep it to people within the organization." Jonah replies.

"Any space or system performance trade-offs?" asks Marcus.

Jonah leans back taking a second look at Marcus and grins "Look at you, Mr. IT man! Good questions and the answer is no and no."

"Have you checked it with Henry?" continues Marcus.

Jonah grimaces, "No, but I think I can get him to go for it on a trial basis. He's not the one I'm worried about, It's Mike I can almost hear him now griping that people will just use it as a reason to slack off and avoid work."

"Yeah maybe your right," Marcus replies "but you got to remember Mike has more people than any of us to keep track of."

Jonah looks off and nods, "yeah, I guess that's true."

Marcus starts to get up to leave, "Well if Henry and Mike are good with it, I'm guessing the rest won't mind.." Marcus stops in his tracks, "I almost forgot, what about Vicki?"

Jonah leans back in his chair, "You know, somehow, I don't think she'll mind. She doesn't seem like the micro-managing type. By the way, what's your initial thoughts on her?"

Marcus pauses "On her, well..she.. certainly seems a lot calmer than Scott!"

Jonah laughs, "Ha! You got that right. It seems Scott only had one speed – hyper!"

Marcus chuckles and starts walking off, "Alright man, let me know what they decide." He waves by and Jonah waves back.

Wednesday, March 14, 3:30

Kisha Wells, 27, is one of Mike's Team Leads. Team Leads may, as the title implies, lead project or line teams. While they are not yet Supervisors, they are seen as having potential. She's temporarily in charge of the Assembly operation and the 20 people in that area. Anthony Viggiano, one of Solons best supervisors left for another job. According to Mike Sessions it was because of a better opportunity, but people on the floor know that Mike and Anthony didn't get along and Anthony didn't seem to respect Mike. Victor has asked Kisha to stop by his office for a quick chat. She comes in and sits in the chair closest to the door. In her view the less time she spends with HR the better. Victor means well she has found, but sometimes he gets overly involved in the interpersonal squabbles that are a part of any workplace.

"Hey Victor.." Kisha says guardedly, "What can I do for you?"

"Close the door Kisha will you." Victor replies solemnly.

As Kisha looks behind her and pushes on the door she closes her eyes for a moment thinking *this can't be good*! She turns around and waits.

"Kisha, I've gotten word that one of your people was upset about what she perceived as lax supervision around safety issues in the assembly area." Victor begins.

"Let me guess, Lisa Williams, am I *right*?" Kisha says her voice rising.

"Well…yes" Victor pauses, "I know she is not one of our star employees, but that's no excuse for not keeping to safety standards."

"Now hold on a second Victor, first of all did she come to you directly?" Kisha asks.

Victor replies, "Well no, she talked with Amanda, but.."

"Again with the going to Amanda," Kisha interrupts throwing her hands up in the air and dropping them in her lap in frustration. "Why is she getting in the middle of this?"

"Look I'm sure she was just trying to be responsive." Victor soothes.

"This is the second time in the last month she came to you before talking to me." Kisha groans wanting to scream.

"Okay, Okay," Victor pleads starting to get uncomfortable. "Do you want me to sit down with the two of you?"

"No!" Kisha replies emphatically. "I will talk to her and to Lisa. Just please, in the future, if you could, ask Amanda to come talk to me first, Okay?" Kisha gets up to go.

"Okay Kisha. But please, drop me a note after you've talked with them and let me know how it goes." Victor replies.

"I'll let you know" Kisha calls out as she as she heads out the door.

Friday March 16, 4:00 p.m.

Vicki is in her office at her desk checking e-mail. It has been a long, but productive week. Vicki found her ride-alongs with the sales and marketing folks very enlightening. To a person she found them knowledgeable, passionate about Solon's products and none too shy with their opinions on how things between Sales and Marketing and the plant could improve. Henry is due at any minute. It is the first time they have had a chance to meet live since Monday.

Henry knocks on the doorjamb and enters. "Hey Vicki."

"Hey Henry, C'mon in and have a seat." Vicki replies.

Henry takes another step forward, then stops and takes note of the changes in the office layout. Vicki has moved her desk so it is against the wall at one end instead of the middle of the room where there is now a small round table with 4 chairs around it. On the wall where Mike had his pictures and certificates and what not, there is now one long whiteboard with some notes and musings and questions in Vicki's scrawl.

"This is *different*" Henry observes.

Vicki spins around in her chair to look at Henry, "Yes, it was a little too cluttered in here before for me."

Henry, curious now, "What's with the desk against the wall?"

Vicki pauses, "Well…you know, I hate having a big desk between me and a person who comes into my office. It just gets in the way. And I find that the small round table seems to make people more comfortable. I try to remember that most people who come into my office, are, because of my position, already a little on edge."

Henry's eyebrows raise and he nods "Hmm, Okay. Where do you want to go over this stuff?" Henry lifts the stack of reports he holds in his hand.

"Lets move the table here a little closer to the whiteboard and sit there. I have some notes and ideas up here I want to refer to." Vicki replies.

As they get settled Henry asks, "Where do you want to start?"

"Let's start with product issues, I've got to tell you, my meetings this week with Sales and Marketing were very enlightening. While it takes a lot of time and is bit of a grind, I always come away from those discussions feeling glad I did it. Even when what they had to say was hard to hear." Vicki replies.

"Yes, those Sales folks can be a little harsh sometimes." Henry empathizes.

Vicki continues, "You're right, but I try to remember where that passion comes from. One thing I learned this past week is that these people care about the quality of product we put out there. They really believe in the 'energy cause', so to speak."

"That's good to hear." Henry says.

Vicki continues "Anyway, let's start with the 770 panels and go from there. According to the Sales folks I met with, our product issues may be more important than we realize. What they wanted us to remember is that what might seem a minor issue to us becomes a major one for customers because for many of them, this is new technology and anything new and unfamiliar is scary."

"New! this stuff's been around for 30 years" Henry snorts.

"Yes, but still for most of our customers, solar is new. It seems we tend to forget that." Vicki replies. "So what's going on with the 770's?"

Henry hands Vicki some papers and they both bend down to look over some data…

An hour or so later…

Vicki and Henry are still going over some data when Vicki looks at her watch, "OK, Henry, it's almost 5:00, it's Friday, You and I have both had a long week, I think we're good for now." She gets up and heads back to her desk and sits down, continuing "How about we get together for thirty minutes before the staff meeting Monday and we can confirm what we need to cover there?"

"OK, sounds good." Henry stands and starts to organize his papers when he suddenly stops and looks down for a second. Feeling a little more comfortable with Vicki now, "Uh, Vicki, can I ask you something about the staff meeting this past Monday?" he says a little sheepishly.

Vicki anxious to get going is tempted to keep getting ready to leave, but stops when she sees that Henry looks a bit uncomfortable. She sits down in her chair again and faces him, "Sure Henry, what is it?"

"I think you caught us all a little off guard when you told us on Monday that you'd be out all week, and that I should continue to run things." Henry stops and looks, but Vicki just waits for him to continue. "Anyway, we" looks down then looks back up "I should say, *I* was wondering if that was some sort of test?"

Vicki, happy that Henry feels comfortable enough to ask a tough question like this, hides a small smile, "No Henry, that was not meant to surprise or be a test. I truly needed to be out in the field for my own education and I really felt that you could handle things as you had been."

Vicki looks off in deliberation for a moment, looks up and says, "Henry, if you got two more minutes I want to tell you something else." She motions for Henry to sit and he does.

"One of the other things I found out this week from the Sales folks is how highly they think of you. Even though they have their gripes, to a person they said they appreciated how flexible the plant has been in responding to emergency changes and to calls for last minute installation support."

She continues, "Now I know it's not news to anybody that Rolf wants to get us to a point where we're positioned to expand operations and eventually go public. One of the things they want to see is that we get our processes and product issues worked out here so we can set up another manufacturing site on the east coast. It's no secret the Governor of New Jersey is pushing hard for some federal dollars so he can bring some clean energy manufacturing jobs to his state." She pauses for effect and waits for Henry to make eye contact, "The feeling is Henry, that *you* might be the person to head up that plant, assuming that you want it, and if all goes according to plan."

Henry's eyes register shock, "Wow, that's great!" he ponders for a moment, "How soon are they thinking about that other site?"

"Hard to say. It partly depends on how hard the Governor pushes for it, but the earliest would be a year, probably two" Vicki replies.

Henry is quiet and Vicki can see that it's a bit much to digest right now. "That's quite a bit away yet, so let's just keep that between you and I for now. There's a lot that needs to happen before we move on that, but I wanted to let you know how you're thought of here by a lot of people and nothing *I* have seen so far contradicts their view." she says reassuringly.

Henry blushes a bit and says "Uh, thanks Vicki."

She gives him a big smile, and gets up saying, "De nada, now get out of here and enjoy your weekend."

Monday, March 19 8:05 a.m.

Vicki and her team are sitting in the large conference room around the table. Also present is Sean Mullen. Sean is an independent management consultant out of the Sacramento area who has worked with Vicki off and on over the past 8 years. Vicki e-mailed Sean's profile to the group over the weekend letting them know he would be facilitating the Leadership Assimilation.

Vicki opens, "Morning everyone and thanks again for being on time. I had a very enlightening experience last week with Sales and Marketing and I'll share with you some of my thoughts around that later in the meeting. Depending on how this assimilation process goes, I'd like to take a short break at the end of it and then have a quick staff meeting. Sound good?"

Looking around and seeing nods, Vicki continues "I think Sean has met everyone and I invited Sean in to take us through this process. As the new person, I'm guessing you have lots of questions so please ask. Sean will go over the process in more detail after I leave the room."

Vicki leaves and Sean gets up to explain what will happen "Hey everyone, again the goal of this process is to accelerate your comfort level with Vicki and she with all of you. As leader, she understands that there are probably some questions you want to ask, but may not feel comfortable asking them yet, so this process allows you to do that. On your handout you will see timeframes for the process and seven questions."

Vicki's Leader Assimilation

1) Vicki leaves and people post their questions (:30)
2) Sean clarifies questions with group (:15)
3) Vicki comes back in and answers questions/Sean facilitates (~ 2 hours)

Questions:

- What do you already know about Vicki?
- What do you not yet know but would like to know?
- What does she know about the team (your understanding)?
- What do you want Vicki to know about the team?
- What do you think are the key challenges facing Vicki over the next 12 months?
- What are your expectations of her?
- What do you think will make Vicki effective in meeting your expectations?

Sean continues, "You will notice that some of the questions are there to unearth any misperceptions that might be out there, like questions 1 and 3. Other questions like # 2 and #6 are there to speed up transparency and candor. You will also see that each question is posted on a flipchart and they are spread around the room. In a minute I'll ask each of you to grab a marker and mill around posting questions or comments as you see fit. My goal after you're done is to help translate the intent of the questions when Vicki comes back in the room. I am *not* here to tell her later who specifically asked what. That is not the game here. Any questions?"

Seeing no questions, Sean continues, "Okay, let's get started…"

Monday, March 19 12:30 p.m.

Sean and Vicki are sitting around the round table having lunch in her office. The Leadership Assimilation ran a little long because the group had a lot of questions and Vicki and Sean decided in the moment to let it go long because the candor and energy was high. Vicki pushed the regular part of the staff meeting back to 4:00 this afternoon. She wants to get Sean's read on the group and on how he felt the process went.

Vicki takes a bite of her sandwich and mumbles, "So, what did you think?"

Sean, ever the consultant, replies, "You tell me, what did *you* think?"

"I thought it went pretty well. I was surprised at the amount of questions around the personal stuff." She replies.

"Really?" Sean replies, "I can tell you from my experience that's not unusual at all. People are dying to know the personal, but often feel its out of bounds, so when they get the chance, they pounce. I thought you would like that?"

Vicki takes another bite of her sandwich, "No, you're right, I see that as a good sign. I want them to feel comfortable around me, and I around them frankly." She acknowledges. "Any observations on my team?"

Sean considers for a moment. "Well, bearing in mind it was only a few hours, here are my thoughts for what they're worth. Amanda was quiet so I don't have much there. Mike…hmm..Mike strikes me as…*shifty*. I'd keep your eye on him."

Vicki gives a knowing nod and grimace to that.

Sean continues, "Victor strikes me as having one foot out the door."
"Yes, but for now, I think I'll have to be content with that. He's got so much company knowledge and history I don't want to lose." Vicki counters.

Sean continues, "OK… now Jonah, I kind of like. He comes off as a bit of a goof off, but he strikes me as being very smart. Marcus seems solid. He may be a little too focused on his own area, but given what's going on right now, maybe that's a good thing."

"Yes, I need him to keep a laserlike focus on our clean room situation right now. What about Henry?" Vicki asks.

"Henry certainly seems capable and people seem to respect him. I'm getting this vibe from him that he still trying to figure out his place. Does that make sense?" Sean asks.

Vicki smiles, "Yes, I think you've hit it on the head. That's partly my fault, in hindsight I may have given him mixed messages so I shouldn't be surprised he's confused, but I think we'll get it figured out."

Vicki continues, "Who does that leave…let's see..oh yes, Sam!"

"Sam, yes…he didn't say much, but he did seem to enjoy hearing you talk about your family and personal interests. He seems like he has more going on than he wants to show." Sean concludes.

Vicki responds, "Yes, I think he could give us much more but he's close to retiring and I'm getting the impression he does not want to exert himself too much in his final days." She ruminates for a moment tapping her pen on the table. "*Now*, let's talk a little bit about what we might do down the road to challenge the rest of the employees…"

At the same time Vicki and Sean are meeting..

Mike is having lunch with his supervisor team: Ryan Sacco, 26, has been the supervisor over the Commercial product line for one year; Hector Maldanado, 30, has been in charge of Residential products for 3 years; Vijay Patel, 28, Delivery and Installation Supervisor for 2 years and Kisha Wells, Team Lead and temporary supervisor for Assembly. They are combining lunch with their weekly production meeting and are wrapping up the items for this week.

"OK, so Kisha, do you need any help with the Diamond Labs job?" Mike asks.

Kisha looks down at her production schedule, "No, I think we're good for now." She replies.

"OK, let me know as soon as possible if you do, we have a tight delivery schedule this week. Oh, by the way, did you get that situation with Amanda worked out? Victor was asking me about it." Sean asks raising one eyebrow as he looks toward Kisha.

Kisha's eyes bug out as she thinks to herself, *Goddamn that Victor! Who else has he told?* "I've sent her two e-mails and haven't heard back from her!" she declares.

"Well get with her and get it resolved! and while we're on it, make sure you keep Lisa under control. I don't understand why the two of *you* can't get along." Mike says with some irritation.

The other supervisor's stop and look at each other and Kisha's face freezes as she absorbs Mike's comment. *Oh he did not say what I think he just said! Please tell me he's not saying we should be able to get along because we're both black!* She is thinking.

"I plan on talking to her too." Kisha replies, thinking to herself, *Man, I need to get on top of this fast.*

Attempting to alleviate the awkwardness, Hector asks Mike, "What was that Leadership Assimilation thing all about?"

Mike shakes his head and says dismissively, "Mostly a bunch of kumbaya stuff. Is there anything else we have to go over?" Mike starts to get up.

"Have you had a chance to ask Henry about those new UL labeling guidelines?" Vijay asks, "I think they could end up causing a lot of headaches for us if we don't get involved with that and find out what's brewing."

Mike is getting agitated. He thought he clarified this already with Vijay. "Look, as far as I'm concerned, it's not even worth bringing up yet. The guidelines have not been approved yet, so no need to worry about it!" Mike starts to head off.

"But.." Vijay starts, and stops when he sees Mike fix him with a stare. Vijay holds up his hands and, chastened, looks down at the table saying "Okay, Okay."

Monday, March 19 4:00 p.m.

The management team is assembled in the conference room for their rescheduled weekly meeting. There is a noticeable increase in energy and interaction as a result of the assimilation process from this morning. Vicki takes notes of that and smiles to herself. It was risky sharing all that information about herself, especially the personal stuff, but she knows from experience it makes her more approachable and the environment more personal.

Vicki starts, "OK everybody, thanks again for being flexible with your schedules today, and I also appreciate the way you all participated in the assimilation process this morning. I've found it helpful to check what's out there about me vs. what's reality as well as have a chance to clarify expectations. My goal is to have some time set aside at each of our weekly meetings to step back and look at how we're operating on a big picture level, and not spend 100% of our time just talking about current orders and quality issues. Does that make sense?"

Mike responds, "Can you give us an example Vicki?"

Vicki continues, "Well…, for instance Mike, in your area, you have people dedicated to the 4 areas, Commercial, Residential, etc. and that probably makes sense in the short-term. But what I would like to see over the long-term is that all those people are rotated through all four areas so they can work in any area on a given day depending on the need."

Mike breathes in and looks around the room for reaction, "But that will take a lot of time to cross-train those people and how do we do that and make sure we're getting our current orders out the door?"

"Great question Mike and I think you've framed it perfectly. That's what we have to figure out. In fact, I'm not even sure we, as in us in this room, should be figuring that out."

Henry, curious now, asks "What do you mean Vicki?"

"What I mean is that I've always felt that any answers to a 'how' question, like 'how do we cross-train and continue to meet daily goals?' should be taken to and answered by the people who have to make it work, and that is often people not in this room." Vicki explains.

"I'm still not sure I'm following..!" Mike retorts. Mike is thinking, *This lady is out to lunch. This will cause chaos and my people are finally comfortable doing what they do now.*

Vicki is starting to wonder now if Mike is going to be able to understand the shift in thinking she wants to see occur, "What I mean is that instead of us sitting in here figuring how to make that happen, Mike, I would say you need to take that question to your group and let them come up with their own answer."

Vicki gets up and moves to the whiteboard, "Look, maybe this is a good time to share with you a simple model and philosophy I've been following for a while that helps me remember how to organize and engage a group around a task."

She writes the following on the whiteboard.

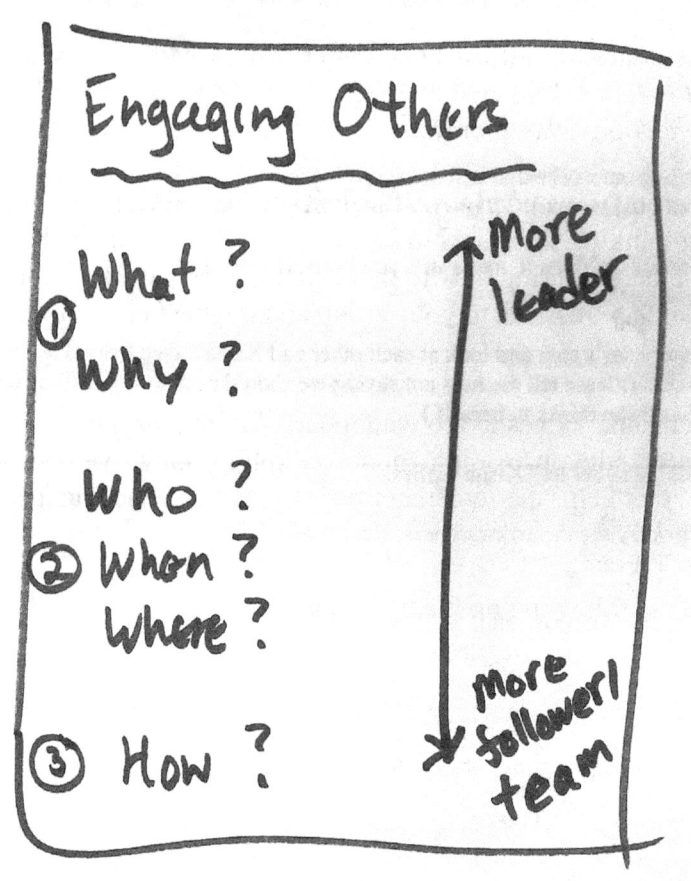

She sits down again and continues, "Now, whenever I sit down with a group or even one person to assign a task, I try to make sure I follow this simple thought process in discussing what needs to be done. That is, I want to make sure I explain *what* needs to be done and *why* before moving into any particulars around *who* needs to be involved, *when* it needs to be done and *where*, and that *what* and *why* piece is a good example of a 'go slow to go fast moment'; meaning I don't want to rush into details about the assignment until everyone is with me on *what* it is we're trying to do and *why* it's important. Does that make sense?"

"It does Vicki, but, you know, a lot of times people don't care about the *why* and just want to be told what to do." Marcus counters.

"I'm not sure I agree with that Marcus. I won't argue that *some* people are like that, but I think that *most* want to know *why*. Don't you like to know *why*?" Vicki looks directly at Marcus and waits.

"Yeah, I guess I see your point." he relents.

Vicky continues, "Anyway, I think we're all guilty sometimes of forgetting that people need to understand that connection to the bigger picture and we help them with that by taking the time to explain the why, and, *yesss* it takes a little longer to do that, that's why I say it's a "go slow to go fast" moment."

Vicki feels like she may be doing too much preaching now, "Anyway, I think the other important point is that as we move down the process to step 3, this is where we need to start pulling ourselves out of the conversation and letting the people come up with their own *how*."

Mike rolls his eyes at this, but Marcus beats him to the punch, "OK Vicki, but same thing again, some people don't want to think and just want to be told!"

Vicki feels herself starting to get annoyed with Marcus's pushback, but then reminds herself that this candor is a good sign. She offers a small smile saying, "Again, I won't argue that some people are that way, but I think it's a small percentage. I think most people like to be given the freedom to do things their own way and unless we have a very compelling business reason against it, we should resist the urge to dictate means. I think we need to remember that how someone does their job is one of the ways people get to express who they are at work."

Mike can no longer hold his tongue, "Listen, Henry and I can't have all 80 people in our area running around doing whatever they please. There are certain process standards that are there for a reason!" He looks to Henry for support.

Seeing this, Vicki opens the door, "Henry?"

"I see what you're saying Vicki, but Mike is right. There are certain standards in place to ensure a consistent product that we don't want people deviating from." Henry responds.

Vicki is simultaneously frustrated with Mike and Henry's inability to grasp what's she's saying *and* happy to see the candor in their questions. She takes a breath and responds, "You're right Henry, and in *those* cases we *do* want consistency and don't want people doing whatever they want. The broader point I want to make is that if we want to more fully engage people in this facility, one of the simplest ways to do that is to a) remember to take the time to explain *why* and b) where possible give them as much leeway as possible around *how*. And certainly I need to model that with you, so as we go forward, if *I* haven't explained the why behind a request or am being too prescriptive around *how*, please let me know. Does that make sense?"

Seeing mumbles and nods, Vicki moves things along, "Let's just let this sink in for a bit. I'm sure many of you may probably follow this process already," pointing to the whiteboard, "I offer it as something we can all try to be more conscious of." She pauses to transition, "Now... that was good discussion and I appreciate the candor. I think that's a good sign. We are definitely not going to agree on everything and I think it helps when we are transparent around where are thinking is coming from. So, unless there's more on this," she looks around the table, "let's get back to the agenda. Henry, why don't you go through this week's order status?"

Henry nods and starts into the discussion on current orders, while he does, Vicki sits back in her chair to assess the team for a moment thinking, *that didn't go too badly, Henry, Jonah and Marcus all seem to sense where I was going with that. I don't know where Mike is, Victor will go with the flow.* Suddenly her thoughts and eyes zero in on Amanda. *What is up with Amanda? She didn't say a word during the meeting and she seems like she's in another world.* She makes a note in her pad, *Amanda?* and circles it.

"..Vicki?" Henry is asking. She snaps out of her reverie and realizing she's not been paying attention says, "Sorry, I was noodling on something else." Henry looks around at the others for a moment then repeats, "We were wondering what corporate is doing about the recent power rating guideline changes Oregon just passed?"

Vicki makes a not on her pad, "I don't know but I'll follow up with Legal to find out."

Henry pauses and looks at Vicki to make sure she is reengaged. Seeing this, she responds, "Sorry, I'm good now, go ahead."

Mike leans his head back and looks up at the ceiling thinking, *Oh man! She's a flake!*

Tuesday March 20, 8:20 a.m.

Marcus is watching Sam up on a ladder replacing the filters in the clean room. He is making a notation in the maintenance log for Sam.

Sam calls out, "Hey Marcus, I don't know if you've noticed, but to maintain are air quality in here we're now having to replace these filters every three months!"

"Yeah I can see that." Marcus replies indifferently not bothering to look up from the book.

As he works on the filters, Sam continues, "What I'm saying is that I'm pretty sure we can get filters that can do just as good a job and only need to be replaced every 9-12 months. These are Aerodyne filters so they're good, but they are also expensive. That's 10 filters every time at what, 150.00 a piece?"

Marcus clearly does not want to get into this with Sam, "No, I get a very good volume discount with Aerodyne so we can afford to change them every 3 months." By his tone he is trying to tell Sam to let it go.

 "Yeah, OK, but you know we have to close the room down for about 4 hours every time and that can add up to a lot of downtime for the line." Sam says mostly under his breath. Marcus hears it but does not respond.

Tuesday March 20, 4:15 p.m.

Amanda is in her office working on some spreadsheets when Kisha appears at her door. "I need to talk to you for a few minutes!" Kisha announces firmly.

Amanda is startled and jumps in her seat. She gathers her composure. She does not like to admit it, but she's a little intimidated by Kisha's straightforward manner. She knows what Kisha is here about, but does not want to deal with it right now.

"I'm kind of in the middle of something here Kisha." She replies.

"Well you won't answer my e-mail so you left me no choice." Kisha replies assertively. She stays put in the doorway with her arms folded.

Amanda, trying to get the upper hand in the situation, turns in her chair and sits behind her desk and motions Kisha to have a seat. She folds her hands on the desk in front of her asking, "OK, what is it?"

Kisha in no mood to dance puts it out there, "I want to know why you went to Victor about Lisa instead of coming to me first!"

"Well Kisha, I don't think I have to justify my actions to you, but if you must know, I'm required to keep HR informed of any possible safety violations." There is a palpable increase in tension in the small office now.

Kisha leans forward in her chair "But you haven't even talked to me about it yet. You only have one side of the story."

Amanda stays firm and folds her arms now, "I'm still required to take action and treat each report of a potential incident seriously. I was going to talk to you about it, but haven't had a chance. Now the best thing you can do is fill out an incident report explaining what happened, and then we can discuss it."

"Why can't we discuss it first? I think you'll see there's no need to start an incident report once you hear what happened!?! Kisha implores.

"That's not the protocol, Kisha. You need to fill out an incident report and I'll compare it with what Lisa says and go from there." Amanda counters. This is not exactly true, but Amanda feels painted into a corner and does not want to back down with Kisha.

Kisha feeling too frustrated for words now gets up to leave and fires back angrily, "Fine, but do me a favor and next time Lisa or *any* of my people come to you with something, come tell *me* before you bring it to Victor!"

Kisha leaves before Amanda can respond. Amanda grabs the armrests on her chair, looks up, closes her eyes and exhales thinking *Ugggghhhh! I don't need this right now!*

Friday, March 23, 4:20 p.m.

Vicki and Henry are sitting in Vicki's office going over the week. They have found it helps to review the week together and make plans for next week in these meetings. Henry is wrapping up discussion on some order trend reports Vicki asked him to put together.

"I took a look at the trends over the last 7 years," Henry says showing Vicki the graph. "and as you guessed we're now selling 80% of our residential panels through Integrators and our costs have been rising faster than our ability to maintain our margins. I assume this is not new news to Sales and Rolf?"

"No." Vicki replies, "they've known about this trend. Unfortunately, Integrators are starting to get the upper hand now that the industry is growing and differentiating. The only reason we're continuing to serve that market is because some of our bigger Commercial Integrators still want to maintain their residential business. They are hoping it takes off given the current administration's energy focus."

Vicki is quiet for a moment and lost in her own thoughts. As if reading her mind, Henry says, "People are not going to be happy if we start getting out of the residential business."

"I know, but I don't think we have much choice." Vicki concludes.

"How are you going to tell people?" Henry inquires.

Vicki steeples her fingers and rests her chin on top of them in contemplation. "I think we need to tell everyone sooner rather than later. I'll let them know at the plant-wide meeting next week."

"There's one last thing." Henry continues, "I think you were copied on some of those e-mails flying around between Amanda, Kisha, Mike and Victor, correct?"

Vicki sits back and rolls her eyes, "Yesss, what is *that* all about?"

"Amanda and Kisha had some kind of falling out and they're trying to resolve it via e-mail. It's getting kind of nasty," Henry says with some disdain.

"I know that Kisha can rub some people the wrong way, but I kind of like her directness. She calls it straight and will be the first to admit when she gets something wrong. I wish more of our people were like that frankly. What I *don't* understand is Amanda. What's going on with her. Have you talked to her?" Vicki asks.

"I tried but I got nowhere. Maybe you can get her to open up. I think she might be more open with a female," Henry counters.

Vicki mulls that over for a moment. "Yeah, OK, but I may not be able to get with her until after next week. I'll be meeting with a bunch of our key Integrators most of the week and we have that all-hands session on Friday. Have we made arrangements for everyone to participate?" she asks.

"We're working on it. Mike is not happy about having to adjust production around having everyone off the line for a half day. Are you sure you want to involve everyone?" Henry asks.

"Yes, we can't say we need everyone's hearts and minds going forward and then exclude people from the conversation. What we *don't* get in terms of bold ideas we'll get in commitment because they will be involved in the decision-making." Vicki says confidently.

"Is Sean going to be running the show?" Henry asks.

"Yes! if any of us are up there running it, I'm afraid people will be sitting there thinking 'Okay, what are you going to foist on us this time?'" Vicki responds. "I really do not want to send that message with my first all-hands meeting. This will be the first of what I hope are many instances where we engage people in a conversation rather than talk at them. Sean has a process he will take us through that may be new for folks, but better, I think. He's going to stop in to go over the process with us on April 4th. Tanya will figure out what time works for everyone. OK?" Seeing Henry's hesitancy Vicki says, "You will just have to trust me on this Henry."

Henry nods thinking, *I don't know about this, I can see it very easily turning into a huge bitch session!*

Wednesday, April 4, 3:10 p.m.

The management team is meeting in the main conference room with Sean. Sean is walking the team through the Open Space process he will be taking the entire plant through on Friday. Vicki takes advantage of Sean leading and observes her team. She can pretty much tell by watching that about half of them (Sam, Jonah and Henry) are mostly open to see how this all plays out, and the other half (Marcus, Mike and Victor) are mostly going through the motions. Amanda seems her usual distracted self. *Damn*, Vicki thinks to herself. *I have GOT to remember to sit down with her and find out what's up.* Vicki tunes in again as she realizes Sean is getting to an important point in the process.

"…So, once Vicki has given everyone the 'state of the union' and I've explained the goals and the process, I have everyone sit in a big circle, I put some blank sheets of paper and markers in the middle and I officially open the floor for people to nominate topics they would like to talk about." Sean explains.

"Not *any* topic, correct?" Jonah checks.

"No, that's right Jonah. Any topic *as it pertains* to the challenges Vicki will be laying out in her presentation."

"What if none of the employees get up to nominate?" Mike asks.

"They will," Sean assures everyone, "Now, what often happens is some employees wait to see what all of *you* do first and that leads to my only firm rule for this team; when I open the floor for topics – do NOT be the first ones to jump up and nominate a topic. Wait until it looks like there are no more topics coming from employees, and then, if there is something you'd like to convene a breakout discussion around that hasn't already been nominated, feel free to do so. But my experience has been that rank and file employees bring up just about everything that needs bringing up. Now, do you understand why it's important you wait until the rest of the people nominate topics before you do?" Sean asks.

"Because if we jump up first, it just starts to look like only a slightly less direct way for us to drive *our* agenda." Jonah offers.

"Exactly!" Sean exclaims.

"But what happens if you nominate and no one shows up for your breakout?" Jonah asks.

"I can see that happening in your case Jonah." Marcus teases.

Everyone chuckles at this including Sean. Jonah responds by holding his thumb and forefinger against his forehead in the universal "loser" gesture toward Marcus. Sean waits for the laughing to subside.

"Well, what that is, Jonah, is feedback for that person that he or she didn't make a compelling enough case for their topic or that people felt other topics were just more important to them. Either way, they usually get the message and end up joining another group." Sean explains.

Marcus asks, "So what happens at the end? Who takes responsibility for following up on the ideas that come out of this?"

Sean responds "Well, the short answer is not you! Meaning, you, as the management team should *not* be taking responsibility for follow up unless it's related to a breakout that you convened. I think the conveners intuitively understand that follow up happens because the people who came to that breakout *want* to follow up, not because they were *told* to follow up. What you as management can do is give them some space and time to follow-up on their ideas."

Marcus is still not convinced, "But what's to stop them from saying they can't get to all their regular production tasks now because they're working on this other stuff?"

Sean opens his mouth to respond, but Vicki waves him off, "Let me handle that one Sean," facing everyone she continues, "First of all, my experience is that 'other stuff' we're talking about is usually production-related. They may be taking time to rethink a process and make it simpler. A classic 'go slow to go fast' thing that involves taking some time to slow down and reexamine what we're doing, but saves time later when we simplify something. The other thing I think we need to be firm about is that while we want to be supportive of new ideas or experiments they want to tryout, that cannot be at the expense of daily production needs. They will have to figure out a way to do both." Vicki says firmly. She looks around the room with a stare that says *this is not up for debate*. She continues, "I know that may come off as kind of harsh, but I want employees to be clear that if we give them more freedom to be more involved and engaged, that with that freedom comes a higher level of accountability and less hand-holding. Comprendes?"

Mike has kept quiet but can no longer contain himself, "But what are we supposed to say when they ask us how do we fit in time for these 'experiments' *and* still get our daily work done."
"Again Mike, great question, but I don't think we need to figure that out for them." Looking at the whole group Vicki continues, "This is what I mean by employees being more accountable as a price for more involvement. What *they* need to do is figure out how they can do both, what we need to do is be flexible when they come to us with suggestions on how they can do both. As long as they are meeting their obligations, I think we need to give them some flexibility in how they make time for other things. Does that make sense?"

Vicki looks around and sees mostly nods from everyone, but is not surprised to see Mike sit back with his arms folded looking unconvinced.

Thursday, April 5, 6:35 p.m.

Vicki is in her office preparing some slides of data she want to share tomorrow at the all-hands meeting. She is determined not to use too much PowerPoint so she has more time to just talk to people about 'where we are' and 'where we need to be.' The last two weeks have gone pretty well. Last week she joined Ryan on a number of Sales meetings with Solon's biggest Integrator customers and learned much about how they saw the solar energy world and the relationship between manufacturers and Integrators. Ryan has a couple of Integrators very close to signing some long-term volume contracts with Solon. This is exciting news and could provide the impetus Vicki needs to challenge the plant to rethink much of the way they do things. Henry in the meantime had his hands full making sure day-to-day operations kept moving along, but he seems to relish the challenge and the chance to show he can be a plant manager. Most everyone is gone for the day so Vicki is a bit surprised to hear the ding of an internal e-mail and sees it's from Amanda about some OSHA stuff. This makes her pause as she realizes, she still hasn't caught up with Amanda yet. Something in her gut says she should do it before the big meeting tomorrow. She gets up and heads to Amanda's office to try and catch her.

Poking her head into Amanda's office she's sees she is on her computer. "Hey Amanda, what are you still doing here?"

"Oh, Hi Vicki. I have to get these OSHA reports finished and e-mailed out. I already told Mike I'd be late tonight." She responds.

Vicki looks at her noting how disheveled and pensive she looks, almost as if she's running on nervous energy. "Do you have a couple minutes? I've been meaning to touch base with you."

"uh..sure come on in." Amanda replies somewhat alarmed now.

Vicki pauses and then offers, "How 'bout we go and get some coffee or something in the cafeteria?"

"Okay.. sounds good" Amanda replies trying to put on a happy face..

They head to the cafeteria and Vicki fixes herself a cup of hot tea and Amanda does the same. Vicki heads to a corner table where they can chat undisturbed on the off chance someone comes in. After they get seated, Vicki waits for Amanda to get settled in and make eye contact. Amanda looks up and sees Vicki's look of concern and looks away again.

"Amanda, I know we haven't had a chance to chat much since our first one-on-one so I'm overdue to catch up. How are things?" Vicki asks in a tone of concern.

Amanda looks up and says too fast, "Good, everything's fine" and looks away again. Vicki can tell there's something at the surface looking to come out, and decides just to wait. Amanda can feel her look of concern and finally puts her head in her hand and starts weeping quietly. Vicki sits quietly for a minute and says nothing while Amanda cries.

"I'm, I'm sorry" Amanda sniffles.

"It's okay" Vicki gets up to grab some tissues pausing to put her hands on Amanda's shoulders and giving her a squeeze. This unleashes a new round of tears so Vicki keeps her left hand on Amanda's shoulder while her right rubs the top of her back gently. Amanda starts to settle down after a minute. Vicki hands her some tissues and Amanda blows her nose and dabs at her eyes. Vicki waits quietly and is torn between one impulse that says *God, I'm tired and I want to go home* and another that says *Amanda could use some support right this very moment*. She shakes off the former idea and sits down again and reaches across the table to squeeze Amanda's hand. "OK…what's going on?"

Amanda gives Vicki's hand a squeeze back and flashes her a smile of gratitude. She sits back and looks off for a moment "God! I thought I would be able to handle this better!" she exhales. Vicki waits for her to continue.

"It's my Mom," she begins…

Thursday, April 5, 8:20 p.m.

Vicki and her husband, George are catching a late dinner together at their home in Berkeley. George teaches high school math in nearby Alameda, and her two sons, Victor, 15 and Michael, 11 go to public school in town. They are both in their rooms doing homework. George pours some wine for Vicki as she rubs her neck.

"Tomorrow's the big employee meeting right?" George inquires as he sits down at the kitchen table with her to eat.

"Yes" Vicki sighs.

"Everything ready?" he asks.

She takes another sip of wine, "I think so. The reason I was late tonight was not because of that," Vicki continues, "It's because one of my manager's had a bit of a melt down at the end of the day and needed a shoulder to cry on, literally?"

"Who is it?" George probes.

"Amanda, my Health and Safety manager." Vicki sits back in her chair shaking her head, "She's got a lot going on poor thing." With that she reflects back to their exchange earlier…

> *"It's my mom…she's got breast cancer." Amanda stifles a sob looking off to the side.*
>
> *"Oh Amanda, I am so sorry to hear that." Vicki replies with concern. Vicki stays quiet sensing that Amanda wants to say more.*
>
> *"She had to have a double masectomy a month ago and she's going through radiation right now. My brothers live out-of-state so it's all on me to help out. It's been very stressful!" She sobs. This brings on another flood of tears.*
>
> *Vicki gets up to grab some more tissues from the counter and gives them to Amanda.*

47

"Thanks" Amanda says dabbing at her eyes and composing herself. "I'm sorry, I know I haven't been myself lately."

"No need to apologize, it's certainly understandable. How can I help?" Vicki says soothingly.

"I don't know honestly. It just feels good right now to tell someone." Amanda admits.

"Am I the first person here you've told?" Vicki asks.

"Yes, I thought I would be able to handle it better than I have been." Amanda says in frustration.

"It must have been hard to be holding that in, yes?" Vicki empathizes.

"Yesss!" Amanda says swallowing a sob and sighing. "I know I've been a bit of a bitch lately and I hate that I've been that way."

"I don't think it's anything that isn't fixable." Vicki assures, "but my first question is, what do you want to do about letting the team know what's going on?"

"God, I don't know…I hate seeming weak, especially around the guys!" Amanda laments.

"Oh Amanda," Vicki responds empathetically, "that's not being weak, that's being human. I think you'll be surprised at how supportive and understanding people can be about these things."

"Yeah, I guess, but I have a hard time telling people, especially the team…can you tell them?" Amanda asks in a pleading tone.

"I certainly could Amanda, but I'm wondering if it would be better coming from you?" Vicki replies keeping a level gaze on Amanda.

Amanda relents under her look and admits, "Yeah, you're right, I guess. I should tell them." Amanda looks off as she thinks about bringing this news to the team.

Vicki contemplates whether now is a good time to bring up a related topic and figures the sooner the better. "You know Amanda, I'm wondering if there's another hard conversation you need to have, maybe even sooner than telling the team this news."

Amanda's head shoots up in surprise, "Huh? What do you mean?"

"Kisha" Vicki says again maintaining eye contact with her.

Amanda looks down saying "Oh...you know about that, huh?"

"It seems like the whole plant knows it by now and that's not good. Now, I understand better why you've been on edge, but as the plant manager, the question going through my mind is how do we make this right? What do you think needs to happen?" Vicki asks her.

Amanda can see that while in one moment Vicki can be very empathetic and supportive, in the next she can be as tough as anybody. "I guess I should talk to her" she says resignedly.

Vicki responds, "I think that's a good idea and the sooner the better as in tomorrow before the plant-wide meeting. I think it's pretty safe to say most if not all the plant knows by now you two need to do some repair work. Agreed?"

"Agreed," Amanda sighs not looking forward to a confrontation with Kisha.

As if reading her mind, Vicki offers, "Now I know Kisha can be a little intimidating and she does have a tendency to wear her heart out on her sleeve, but that just tells me that she cares. I don't really know Kisha well yet, but my instincts tell me that once you get past the tough exterior, you'll find she's more bark than bite."

"By tomorrow?" Amanda asks hoping for a different answer.

Vicki is firm, "Yes, I think it will really help the day if the rest of the people see that you two have patched things up. Okay?"

"Okay" Amanda sighs.

Vicki continues, "And listen...regarding your mom...let me know when you've told the team, and please know that if you need to time off or a more flexible schedule, just let us know and I think I can speak for everyone and say we'll do what we need to do to give you what you need. Okay?"

Amanda smiles for the first time since the conversation began, "Yes, and thanks Vicki."

Vicki reaches across the table to pat her arm, "De nada. Now go home and get some rest."

Vicki realizing her husband has just asked her a question snaps out of her reverie, "Huh? What did you say Jorge?"

"I said, Victor's baseball game is 7:00 tomorrow night, under the lights, do you think you'll be able to make it?" George repeats.

"I don't know, probably not. It's just too big a day tomorrow to expect to leave on time." She replies.

George's face register disappointment, "Then you better go tell him. You haven't made a game yet and there are not many left."

"I know, I know" she says a bit defensively, "I told you the first 3-6 months are going to be crazy…"

Friday, April 6, 12:25 p.m.

All of the plant personnel are spread among makeshift tables set up on the manufacturing floor. They are finishing up pizza and salad Vicki had ordered delivered for lunch. There is a screen set up for viewing a presentation at one end of the room and a series of flipcharts scattered here and there. Vicki paid for the food out of her budget as a thank you to everyone for participating in today's all-hands meeting. Vicki made sure that her managers told everyone that attendance was *optional,* not mandatory. She wants employees to remember that they always have choices and choices have consequences. Vicki saw Amanda and Kisha happily talking and eating together. She smiled assuming Amanda and Kisha had talked and resolved their differences. *That's a good sign!* she is thinking.

"Hey, can we get everyone to start cleaning up and moving the tables over by the lunchroom out of the way." Vicki announces loudly.

People start getting up and throwing away trash and moving tables while Vicki goes over by the projector set-up to make sure everything was ready to go. Sean insisted on having a mic available, even though Vicki said she wouldn't need it. Once the tables were put away and most everyone was standing around the floor wondering what's next, Vicki realized the mic would come in handy after all.

"Can I get everybody to grab a chair and form some rows in a semi-circle around the screen up here." She announces using the microphone.

As the group starts to form around her she takes an unofficial headcount and estimates that there are over hundred people in attendance. Tanya offered to handle the phones and a couple customer service people needed to be by their phones, but other than that, it looked like everyone else was in attendance. Once everyone was seated and now closer, Vicki put down the mic and stood in front of everyone. *OK, here we go…*, she thought.

"Afternoon everyone," she announces loudly, "and thanks for adjusting your schedules so we could take an afternoon to do this today. I know this meant some of you will have to squeeze some extra time in next week to stay on schedule and I want you to know we understand that it may mean some overtime for some of you and that's okay."

Some murmurs of approval at this announcement. Vicki explains, "This is the first of what I hope to be more opportunities to engage all of you in a conversation. A conversation about what we're trying to do here and why, and asking all of you to help us figure out how to make it happen. In a minute I'm going to talk a bit about where we are as a business vs. where we need to be and how we need all of you to help us get from here to there. Bear with me as I have a few slides to kind of paint the picture. That should only take about 15 minutes. At that point, I will hand it over to Sean here" she points to Sean who stands up and gives a wave, "to help us with the major part of this workshop which is to take us through a process where given our current challenges, you get to propose topics and actions to address those challenges and convene your own breakout groups to discuss and address them. I truly believe that the people closest to the work, know best how to improve it. So, before I continue, any questions about what we're trying to do or why?"

Vicki scans the room looking for hands even though she knows in this size group most people would be reticent to ask anything.

"Okay" she says and hits the keyboard for the first slide.

Vicki spends the next 15 minutes giving people a sense of what's going on in the industry and the implications for Solon going forward. After explaining some of the trends in the industry, she takes her time sharing her own observations about the strengths of Solon and in particular, the plant. She wants people to feel good about some of their current practices and results before challenging them on some things that need to change going forward. After explaining the trends going on in the Integrator world, and the fact that 80% of Solon's residential product goes through them, she drops the bomb on the group….

"So, given what we see going on, I wouldn't be surprised if we are completely out of the residential business in five years." Vicki pauses to let the grumbling and looks of shock emerge. Instead of backing up, Vicki knows better so she moves closer to the group and puts down the remote for a second.

"That's right everyone," she continues, "I don't like having to say it, but residential is *not* a sustainable option if we want to grow our business and have a national presence. The better opportunity is in commercial and we will need to wean ourselves from the residential business. The only reason we will continue with some aspects is for our large Integrator customers who still want to serve that market, but even they seem to be moving more toward commercial." Vicki stops again to let that sink in and allow the murmuring and side conversations run their course.

"Now… this is the place where we *most* need your help," Vicki emphasizes, "the management team and I do not know how we are going to make that transition. Our costs are still too high and if these two long-term Integrator contracts come through, we will need to rethink many of our current practices. I can tell you right now that Corporate will not support us hiring lots of people if we haven't first looked at simplifying our processes and bringing our costs down. We will need your help to figure this all out. This is still an industry that is emerging and defining itself, so my commitment to you is to give you more information about what's going on and what I need from all of us is more flexibility to better respond to these emerging trends. And that leads to a perfect example of a question that we need your help answering. 'How do we create a reliable product and stay flexible in our approach so we can smoothly transition when we need to?' No one person in this room can answer that, not even Henry," Vicki teases. Everyone laughs at this including Henry who blushes a beet red.

Vicki continues, "That is just one example of the kinds of questions we will be bringing to you to help us collectively answer, and this leads to a couple things I want to talk to about regarding how we work together going forward." Vicki clicks to the slide below…

Effectively Engaging Others

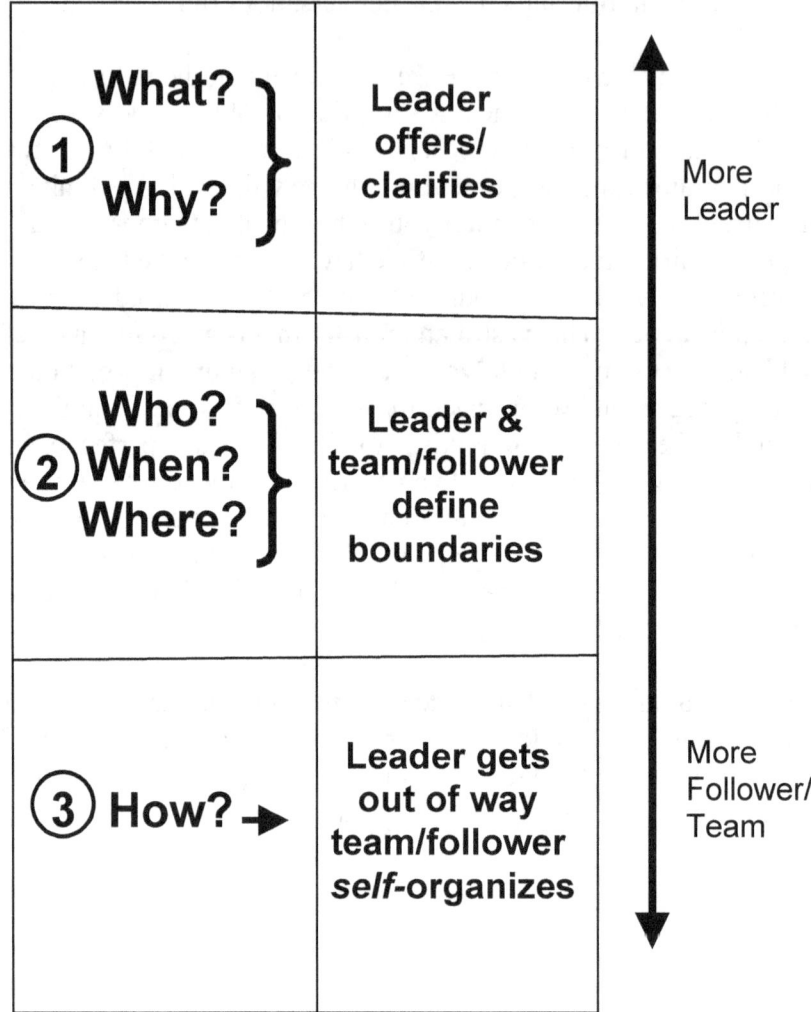

"I've shared this with the management team and asked them to do their best to follow this fairly simple model for engaging others in getting something done." Vicki goes on to explain, "Now, you will see the word 'leader' up there and I want you to know that could be *any* of us. Anytime we try to engage someone or a team in trying to accomplish something, I think it helps if we all follow this thought process. It's pretty intuitive and mostly common sense. For me, it's a reminder that when I ask the management team to help me with something, my first task is to explain *what* I think we're trying to accomplish and more importantly, *why*. As the leader in this case, that first step is mostly on my shoulders. As we move down the model to the next series of questions my role is to have a discussion where we clarify any boundaries or constraints around *when* it needs to be done, *where* and *who* might need to be involved. Lastly, when we get to the *how* question, I think it best if we leave that, as much as possible, up to the people who have to complete the task."

Vicki goes on, "Now this may seem like common sense, but my experience has been it is not common practice. Where I have seen it not be common practice is around the step of explaining "why". Now, I will come back to why that happens in a minute, but I think we should first look at what, I think, constitutes a *legitimate* 'why'. Vicki clicks to the next slide.

5 Legitimate "Why's"

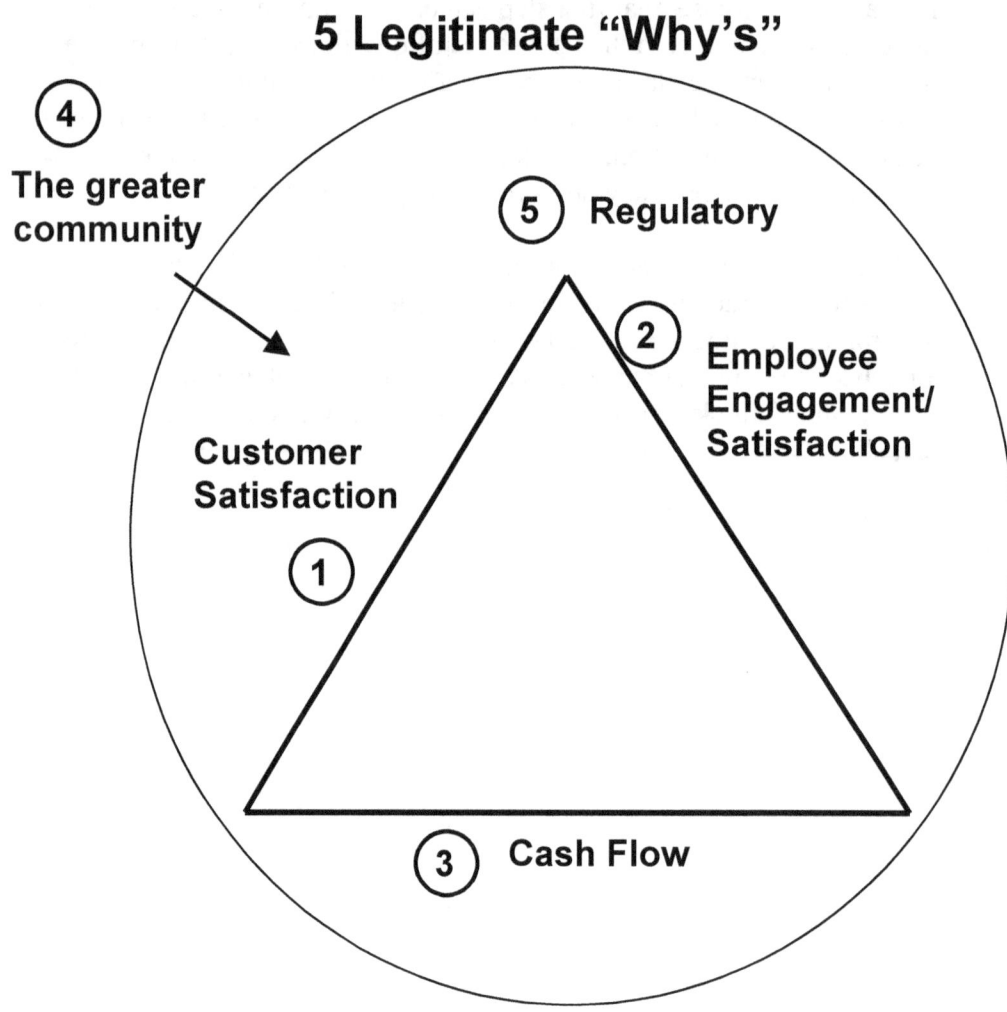

"These are what I feel are legitimate reasons for what we do. When we get people together and talk about the *why* part, I think we need to make sure it is because it's impacting one or more of these five things." Pointing to the screen Vicki continues, "The first three legitimate *Whys* are around the triangle and are probably the easiest to understand. We're doing something because it *adds value to a customer* who is willing to pay for that; it helps us *be more productive* in our work or it *improves our cash flow* situation. The last two are less concrete but also legitimate. We might have to do some things because say, OSHA requires it or because it enhances our image in the community, like the Habitat for Humanity project we do each year. We don't make money on that, in fact, we're giving away our time, but it's a part of being a good community member."

Vicki would like some feedback on all this but knows better than to ask the entire group of 100. She has learned over the years that as soon as you get a group of even just 10 people, asking questions of them rarely leads to candid responses. People are just too scared of saying something stupid in front of their peers and the larger the group, the more reserved people are.

"Now I know that's a lot to digest so what I'd like to do is get some initial reaction to all that. If you would, just form groups of four or five with the people around you and have a some discussion on anything I just covered." She announces.

People start moving their chairs around into smaller groups and very shortly, there is an immediate rise in energy and noise as people start talking about all the things Vicki just went over. Vicki has learned that what people won't feel comfortable expressing in a group of 20 let alone 100, they usually *will* feel comfortable saying in a group of 4 or 5. While the groups are chatting, Sean makes his way over to Vicki and leans in to whisper, "This is going to put us a little behind on schedule."

Vicki nods while continuing to observe the groups chat. "I know, but I wanted to give them a little time with this and I knew if I just asked the entire group if they had any thoughts or questions, I would get next to nothing."

"That's for sure," Sean agrees. "How long do you want to allow for this?"

"I'll give them about ten minutes in the small group and another ten minutes to hear some of what was discussed." Vicki replies.

"Okay, I'll make the adjustments to the timing," Sean says.

The small group discussion is still going strong after ten minutes and Vicki would like to let it go a bit longer, but she doesn't want to eat any more time from the Open Space process. She gets everyone's attention and asks for some questions or comments. Most of what comes out is similar to what her management team brought up previously. Vicki is as candid as possible in answering their questions, and after about 10 minutes of this, she holds her hands up and announces… "Okay, everyone, those were some very good questions and comments and I hate to cut this short, but you will have a chance to go further on this during the Open Space process. So, at this point, I want to hand it over to Sean. For those of you who have not met Sean yet, his bio is in your handout package. Sean and I used to work together at NextGen Fuels and he's helped me out before in his new consulting role."

Vicki turns toward Sean and motions him to take over. Sean steps up and decides to forgo the mic as well. Announcing loudly, "Afternoon everyone! And thanks for participating. I think you'll find this process different than your usual all-hands meetings and I think you will enjoy it. My role is to be the 'keeper of the process.' I can't even say Facilitator because one of you will be taking on that role in your breakout discussions. So once we get rolling, you won't see much of me except to move us from one phase to the next. I won't go into the history of where this Open Space Technology thing came from and don't let the 'technology' word fool you. It is a very low-tech process and much simpler than the title implies. Basically, instead of the usual meetings that you come to which tend to be highly scripted on what's going to be discussed and by who, this process lets *you* decide much of that. In a few moments I'm going to open the floor for people to nominate topics they feel are important to convene around given everything Vicki just went over regarding moving the business forward. Now would be a good time to read over the handout titled *Open Space – Explained.*"

Sean pauses and gives everyone a few minutes to read over the handout. "Now, a couple of things before we get started. You see the butcher block paper over on the wall?" Sean says pointing it out, "that is our bulletin board. You will see we have two time slots each of about 90 minutes, that 90 minutes includes time to identify topics, pick and move to a breakout, discuss your topic and finally, write a summary on a couple flipchart pages. Whoever nominates the topic is the Convener and is responsible for scoping out an area for your breakout and running the meeting. We suggest you solicit help to do things like facilitate, capture key points, keep track of the time, etc. Don't take it all on your shoulders. After each breakout we will have time for everyone to go around and hear a quick summary from each group on what they discussed and where they landed. Some of you after the first round may choose to go even deeper on your same topic in the next round and that is perfectly okay. In the same vein, if you were part of a discussion in round 1 and they are going to continue it in round 2, you are not obligated to go to that breakout again. And that leads to probably the most important principle to remember, *The Law of 2 feet.* If at any point, you are not feeling engaged in the conversation or thought it was going to go in one direction, but find that it's *not,*" Sean pauses for effect, "Then get up and go somewhere else. Find another topic you have some energy for. I have seen people start in one breakout and want to go in a more specific direction under that theme and start a whole new breakout discussion. That is perfectly fine also. Any questions?"

Jonah who is starting to get excited about the process asks, "How will we handle the walking around and hearing from each group piece? A hundred people is a lot to be moving around."

Open Space - Explained

The Concept

- Open Space Technology is a phrase coined by Harrison Owen originator of the process. The process is much simpler than it sounds and is based on people's innate ability to self-organize.

- Given a general theme/topic (e.g., improvements we must make to our products/services) participants decide what topics they would like to discuss and put them on the community bulletin board in a particular time slot.

- Participants then self-select which topic they want to go to based on interest

The Process:

1. Participants write down a topic/question, announce to group and put in an open time slot on the bulletin board until all slots are filled or no other additional topics suggested.

2. Group reviews the topics to combine any where it makes sense and negotiate timing of topics

3. First segment starts with Convener of each group responsible for making sure notes are taken

4. After each segment, notes are summarized on 1-2 pieces of flipchart and posted in community area for all to see.

5. Start next segment, and at all times follow principle of "2 Feet"

The 4 Principles:

- Whoever comes is the right people
- Whatever happens is the only thing that could have
- Whenever it starts is the right time
- When it's over it's over

The Law of 2 Feet

If at any time you feel you are neither contributing or learning from the discussion you are part of, get up and move somewhere else.

"Good question Jonah," Sean replies, "Let's play that by ear and I'll have a better idea once we see how many breakout groups there are. Sound good?"

Jonah nods and Sean looks out over the group again, "anything else?…Okay then, let's put our chairs in a big circle right over here and we'll get started."

People start getting up and moving the chairs around in the open space on the floor. Sean and Vicki purposely sit across from each other and the managers were told to spread around the circle and not sit together. As the last few people start to get settled in the circle, Vicki catches Sean's eye and nods. Vicki knows that we are about to reach what Sean calls the "gulp moment" where everyone waits to see who will be the first brave soul to go up in front of everyone and, in essence, "take a stand."

Sean goes and grabs a bunch of markers and blank pieces of paper and stands in the middle of the circle. "Okay in a moment I will open the floor for people to come up. I suggest you come up, write down the topic nice and big on one of the pages, hold it up and announce loudly what you would like to talk about. Then you go and tape it on one of the breakout slots. Once all the topics are identified, we can all go over to the bulletin board and see if there are any topics that need to be combined or moved to the 2nd round because it needs to follow something discussed in the first round. Questions?" Sean asks. "Okay, the floor is officially open," he announces.

This is the moment that Sean was adamant with the management team about. They must not be the first to jump up with a topic. Almost as a subtle reminder,
he tries to make eye contact with as many of them as possible to give them a nod.

Trying to direct attention away from herself, Vicki sits serenely and looks toward the middle of the circle and closes her eyes. Most of the other managers take her cue and look toward the middle as well. Mike finds himself sitting next to Hector, one of his supervisors. He looks at Hector who just shrugs. Mike just folds his arms and shakes his head thinking *this is for the birds!*

It gets very quiet in the group as almost all the rank and file folks look around the circle at each other. Vicki keeps her eyes closed and prays that somebody gets up soon. After what seems to be an interminable wait, Vijay Patel gets up and moves toward the center and grabs a piece of paper to write. Vicki opens her eyes and breathes a sigh of relief saying to herself *Thank you Vijay!* Vijay holds his paper up and says, "I'm interested in talking about what we need to do to prepare for the new UL labeling guidelines that are coming." Mike sits back and folds his arms again thinking, *he just won't let that go that little SOB!*

As Vijay goes to the bulletin board to post his topic, one of Kisha's people gets up and heads toward the paper in the middle of the circle. *Here we go…!* thinks Vicki excitedly.

"Rules" – Part 1

You don't need a crisis or a huge precipitating event to start down the path of fuller engagement, but it helps. In the story, we see Vicki using the possibility of a couple major contracts as a catalyst to challenge the way things are done at the plant. She freely admits to everyone gathered that neither she or the management team has the answers for how to specifically respond to the challenges. Her candor to admit this brings us to the first rule of engagement for leaders - **admit to your limitations and inability to control things.** This may seem heretical and unleaderlike to many of you, but I don't think you can truly let go and engage others until you do. Leaders who are thriving in these constantly changing and unpredictable times have learned that if they can't admit that, they will burn themselves out quickly. We know from complexity science research and first hand experience that within any large complex system or organization an individual can only influence about 15% of that system.

One thing you may have noticed in Vicki's approach with her team and employees is she is not afraid to take tough questions directly to the line employees and challenge them to come up with sustainable solutions. Many of the really challenging questions we all struggle with at work, including:

- How do we bring costs down and quality up?
- How do pursue short-term profits and invest for the future?
- How do we involve employees more fully in decision-making and be efficient?
- How do we meet our obligations to customer, shareholders, the community and to each other *and* maintain a healthy work-life balance?

all share the same paradoxical quality of seemingly two opposing forces that don't seem to go together (e.g., *short-term* profits and invest for the *future*). These are the challenging questions that can and should be taken directly to employees and you bring accountability into the equation by framing the questions appropriately. By putting both desires in the same question and connecting them with an *and* instead of an *or*, you put employees on the spot to be accountable *and* pay more attention to the whole when coming up with solutions. This brings us to the next rule of engagement – **bring the really tough questions directly to employees AND stop organizing their efforts.**

In Vicki's case, even if she does have an idea, she is wise enough to realize that forcing her idea on the plant in some top-down fashion will only backfire. It does not matter how "right" her idea may be, people will not sustain something they have not had a hand in creating. This is why being flexible around the *how* becomes so important and takes us to the third rule of engagement - **clarify the *what* and *why* but stay out of the *how*.** In my work with new leaders, this is often one of the hardest things for them to address. Very often it is precisely because of their ability to come through on the "how" that got them promoted in the first place. So why are we surprised when they have a hard time letting go of that as managers. For leaders, it does not matter that you *mean well* with your detailed instructions. The more important thing to remember is that the main way people express who they are at work is through *how they do their job*. So, if we want them to more fully engage, we need to give them that space to express themselves via how they go about doing their job.

Giving employees space does *not* mean no boundaries. If anything, the more space you give to play, the more necessary to clearly define boundaries. The problem with defining boundaries is that for far too long, too many managers have followed the rule of maximum specifications instead of "min specs." "Min specs" is another concept that comes from Chaos/Complexity theory. The idea is that whenever trying to provide some amount of structure to a complex system (organization), better to provide the *minimum* number of specifications or rules to allow for *maximum* diversity of approaches from the players within that system. Instead, all too often what we see is management, in an effort to "keep things under control," over-engineer things by trying to outline all possible scenarios and responses for each. This usually ends up being both too cumbersome to be useful and often counterproductive because it drives rote, unthinking behavior. If you take all the decision-making and thinking out of the equation for employees and ask them to just "follow the script", you create conditions where people all too easily go on autopilot. At best this leads to disengagement and apathy; at worst it can lead to major errors. This leads to our fourth rule of engagement – **Take a "min specs" approach when defining boundaries around how people can go about doing their work**. Nordstrom's provides a great extreme example of a min specs approach by having an employee handbook that has one rule "use your good judgment in all situations." You will see other examples of the use of min specs in part two of the story.

The Rules of Engagement

1) **Admit to your limitations in controlling things.**
2) **Bring the really tough questions directly to employees AND stop organizing their efforts.**
3) **Clarify the *What* and *Why* but stay out of the *How*.**
4) **Take a "min specs" approach when defining boundaries around how people can go about doing their work.**

Please note that while I use the term "rules" because it works well as a title for the book, I am really talking about *guidelines*. The second thing to note is that the first two rules speak more to things leaders should stop doing or do less of and the next two are things leaders might do more of instead.

Part 2:

Letting Chaos Do Its Work

"To be a god, at least to be a creative one, one must relinquish control and embrace uncertainty. Absolute control is absolutely boring. To birth the new, the unexpected, the truly novel—that is, to be genuinely surprised—one must surrender the seat of power to the mob below. The great irony of the god games is that letting go is the only way to win."

~ Kevin Kelly, *Out of Control*

Friday September 1, 5:30 p.m.

We are six months into Vicki's tenure as Plant manager and four months since she laid down the charge to the plant in the all-hands meeting. Vicki is at her desk preparing her notes for a conversation for a call with Rolf at 6:00. She is reflecting on and jotting down some of the things that have happened the past few months. On the plus side, there has been a noticeable uptick in energy from employees as they have found Vicki's combination of candor and tact a refreshing change from her predecessor. There has also been a number of skunkworks efforts going on that came out of the Open Space Process. Vicki jots down some of those things on her pad:

- A group looking into the clean room filtering process to see about improvements there with Sam supporting that effort
- Vijay has a small group looking into the UL labeling changes
- Another group has started looking into increasing safety practices in the assembly area and Kisha and Amanda are hard at work in giving those groups time to meet
- One of Henry's engineers is working with a design engineer at Corporate to explore making panels more visually appealing

Vicki is pleased with these efforts and the fact that they all started with employees. She also notes that some of the breakout discussions from that meeting never really took off, but she knows from experience that's part of the price you pay with the process and that ideas that are less viable will wither and die as they should.

The other good news is that Solar Solutions signed a five year purchasing agreement with Solon with a "Review/Renew" process every year. However, the agreement specified volume discounts and cost structures that will force the plant to be even more efficient going forward.

Lastly, Vicki reflects on the overall mood of people at the plant. While employees seem to be warming up to her and seem okay with the fact that she is leaving the daily production responsibilities with Henry, the management team is a mixed bag. On the plus side, Amanda seems renewed. She has let the team know about her situation and they have all in their own way pledged to support her. She is almost like a new person. Jonah, Henry and Sam seem even more supportive, although with Henry he can be encouraged one day and worried the next. Marcus continues to be ambivalent, Victor is still going along and Mike continues to be skeptical although he's politically smart enough not to let it show it too much.

Vicki checks her watch and sees it's almost time to call Rolf. She wonders if Rolf will show patience with what she's trying to do.

Friday September 1, 6:10 p.m.

Vicki is on her office on speakerphone with Rolf…

> *"..that's all well and good Vicki, but I'm not liking what I see re: these cost and productivity numbers for 3nd quarter. We're starting to trend in the wrong direction!"* Rolf exclaims.

"I know Rolf, but it's only been six months and I warned you that it would take a while, and don't be surprised if September's numbers are just as bad. We're just now getting our experiments going with employees and it will take a bit before we see the fruits of those efforts!" Vicki pushes back.

> *"Just don't let it take too long, Vicki. We need to meet those pricing agreements with Solar Solutions and we have SunWorks waiting in the wings to see if we can make this work!"* Rolf admonishes.

Vicki starts to relent under Rolf's barrage, "Okaaaay, I hear you Rolf. We should be able to get those number's back in the right direction by end of 4th quarter."

> *"Now that's what I like to hear Vicki! It looks like I'll be up in your area in a month. We'll catch up then."* Rolf says.

"Sure thing Rolf. Just have Allison contact Tanya when you firm up your plans. Take Care."

Vicki hangs up the phone and stares out her office window thinking, *God, why do I let Rolf push me like that! Now we've got to figure out how to hit those numbers without killing the good stuff.*

Monday September 4, 8:45 a.m.

Vicki and the plant management team are having their weekly team meeting. They have gone over the staffing and production issues for the week and the rest of September, as well as quality issues and goals for the month. Vicki would like to switch gears...

"All right, are there any other immediate issues that we need to cover?" Vicki asks leaning forward and looking around the table.

"Yes, I think we need to figure out what we need to do to keep Vijay under control." Mike responds.

"What do you mean?" Vicki responds.

"Well he's getting a little carried away with his labeling group. He's talking about having a meeting where he wants to invite people from a couple suppliers, somebody from Solar Solutions, plus another Integrator and, on top of all that, a UL rep! Can you believe it!?! Like he has a prayer of getting those people in the same room together." Mike exhorts.

Amanda asks, "Would UL allow one of their people to do that?"

"No way" Mike says shaking his head.

Henry interjects "Actually, they already said yes." There's a collective gasp from the group.

Amanda exclaims, "Really!" and right behind her Mike chimes "No way!" Everyone is looking at Henry now.

"Yep, I saw Vijay this morning and he said he got an e-mail over the weekend saying they are open to sending someone in an advisory capacity only." Henry continues.

Mike is studying Vicki to gauge her reaction and sees her with a slight smile nodding her head at this news.

"Yeah, but we can't have Solar in there with a competitor, we just got that contract. We don't need to do anything to tick them off!" Mike protests.

71

Vicki is about to respond, but sees that Henry wants to so she holds off.

"I asked Vijay about that and he told me he explained all that to the Solar people, and they said they were fine with that. They want to hear about these labeling guidelines as much as anybody and don't see it as a competitive thing. I think this should actually help our relationship with them, because we're making a point of including them." Henry counters.

Mike is flummoxed by all this and doesn't know how to respond. The political animal in him realizes that it's best if he keeps quiet for now.

Vicki offers, "You know. I kind of like that idea. In fact, I think we should extend an offer to each of our key Integrator customers and sell it as an information sharing thing we want to host since it impacts everybody. It would be interesting to see how many show and it might give us an idea of how willing some of our Integrators would be to collaborating more with us, and possibly with each other."

"What do you mean *collaborate with each other*?" Marcus asks

"Well, I don't have a specific idea in mind, but I've found you can almost never go wrong with getting some face time with a customer. There have been many times when I've sat down with customers to discuss one thing, like, in this case labeling, only to find out all kind of other interesting things that come up in the course of conversation." Vicki explains.

"Does he have a date for the meeting yet?" Vicki asks Mike.

"I don't think so." Mike responds.

"Actually, he does." Tanya interjects. Everyone looks at Tanya surprised since she usually doesn't say a word at these meetings. Tanya is looking at a notepad while she continues, "he called me this morning and asked if he could reserve this room for October 27."

Vicki sees that this is news to Mike and that he's starting to get steamed.

"This is what I mean. He's out of control!" Mike says in frustration.

Vicki can't help but put her hand over her mouth to suppress a smile at Mike's discomfort. Pat of her would like to watch him squirm more, but she decides to give him his due.

"Mike, you're right. He probably should have cleared that with you first, but we should all not lose sight of the fact that this is exactly the kind of initiative we were asking for when we put the charge to everyone at the April all-hands meeting. So, while you may need to admonish him a bit, Mike. Don't forget to acknowledge his intent." Vicki replies keeping her gaze on Mike until he makes eye contact with her.

Mike meets her gaze finally and sighs, "Yeah Okay."

Vicki continues, "That leads to the one other thing I wanted bring up today before we break. I spoke with Rolf at the end of the day on Friday, and he was not happy with our cost and productivity numbers last quarter. I was hoping he would be giving us, giving me really, some more time to turn it around, but he's getting impatient."

Vicki pauses and looks around the table noticing that people are bracing for bad news.

"He wants to see us getting those numbers turned around by end of 4th quarter. At least 10-15% better I would say if we want to keep him off our backs." She explains.

Everyone exhales a little at this news as it is not as bad as it could have been. The layoffs were not that long ago. They look at each other wondering who will respond first.

"Well, that's doable I think, but we will probably need to postpone some of these employee initiatives so we can focus everyone on this effort." Marcus responds looking toward Vicki. Mike and Victor nod at this idea, while the others wait for Vicki's response.

"That's just it Marcus. I don't think we can put those things on hold for a couple of reasons. One, we lose credibility with our people if we stop their momentum after we just asked them to step up, and two, what they are working on *will* help our productivity, eventually. It may not be fast enough for Rolf, and, you know, I have to take ownership for not pushing back on Rolf more. That's my fault, but we are where we are and now we need to figure out how to make this happen." Vicki explains.

Marcus counters, "So how are we supposed to hit those numbers next quarter and still support these other initiatives?"

Vicki smiles realizing she has a "teachable moment" in front of her, "What do you think I'm going to say to that Marcus?"

Marcus sees where she is going and decides to play along "Let me guess, *take the question to the employees*." He replies in a singsong fashion.

Most of the team chuckles, while Mike rolls his eyes.

"That's right." Vicki responds, "one reason I left this item until the end is that I didn't want us to try and start answering it here ourselves, but first communicate the challenge to your teams and see what they have to say. We're not saying we're going to do everything they suggest, but that we want to *hear* it and *consider* it and when we get together, next Monday we can go over their ideas then. So you have this week to sit down with your teams to collect their thoughts and bring those with you on Monday, then we can sift through them and add our own to the mix. Comprendes?"

Seeing nods around the table, Vicki ends with "So, just to make sure we're on the same page, I think the question we now want to put to them is 'How do we reach these new productivity goals for next quarter *and* continue to support our open space initiatives *and* meet our weekly production goals?' Sound right?" Vicki asks with enthusiasm. Seeing nods around the table, she starts getting up to leave "Okay let's see what they have to say?"

Monday September 4, 5:20 p.m.

Mike is in his car on his way home from work and is making a call on his cell phone.

"Yes, this is Mike Sessions, do you know if Scott Hastings is still in….he is, great! Could you connect me…thank you. Hello Scott, It's Mike! How you doing man?…Good, good, listen do you have a few minutes…you do, great!..Listen, this is what I wanted to talk to you about…"

Monday September 11, 8:00 a.m.

Vicki and her team are set for their weekly team meeting. Vicki asked them to block an extra hour so they could work through the suggestions brought forward from employees. It was a hectic week last week. The new filters for the clean room that Sam's team is trying out took two hours longer to install than the old type. Some production time was lost, but Sam attributes it to the learning curve and thinks they will be able to get the time down with more practice, plus they will only need to be replaced every 9-12 months instead of every six months. Orders schedules are still on target for the week and month, but there was an increase in errors in Assembly as people were apparently feeling rushed a bit to get everything done last week. Vicki makes a mental note to follow up with Mike on that.

Also in the room is Sean and six employees from different functions in the plant. Sean suggested getting some line people involved in today's meeting to maintain a certain level of transparency and Vicki agreed. Mike didn't like the idea of the lost person-hours and Victor thought this was a bad precedent (inviting line employees into the management meetings) but Vicki overrode them both. As she looks around the table, Vicki can see that people are visibly tired. The extra activity is taking a toll and people are finding it hard to get their typical tasks done and make time for the improvement initiatives. The more Vicki thinks on this, the more she is glad they are having this session today.

"Morning everyone!" Vicki starts, "Thanks for being on time. I know we all have a lot on our plates and I appreciate everyone freeing up an extra hour for today's meeting. Let's welcome Steve, Michael, Trish, Ving, Myla and Ty for joining us," Vicki looks and nods to each of the line employees as she welcomes them. "Sean and I felt it was important to have some line perspective as we go through this exercise today. I first want to say that I know how hard everyone has been working to help us meet our productivity numbers and continue to get product out and improve things. I'm sure many of you are feeling like there's just not enough time in the day."

Vicki sees some grateful nods and continues, "I think the process Sean will be taking us through in just a minute will help us start to examine some of the things we are doing and maybe shed some things that no longer seem to make sense. In hindsight, Sean and I realized that this would have been better placed just before the Open Space process, but better late than never. I think once we go through this together, we can make smarter choices about which ideas and current practices we should continue to support going forward and which we might need to let die. With that said, let me turn it over to Sean." Vicki looks toward Sean and nods.

Sean stands and heads over to stand by a flipchart. "Morning everyone," Sean begins, "What I want to do is walk everyone through a model for growing and sustaining a business and talk about some of the traps that go with that, and then let you work both individually and in small groups to use that model to examine what we have going on here at the plant. Now all of you have a copy of what we call the Ecocycle Planning model for business. It is a way to use nature as a metaphor for thinking about how to grow and sustain your business.

Sean starts to draw what's in their handout on the flipchart page explaining as he goes, "Most of us are familiar with the typical growth curve for businesses represented by the solid part of the figure eight. In the early stages you need the entrepreneurial mindset like the Solon founders Tim and Glenn had. As you move up that growth curve you need a more *bureaucratic* type leader to develop systems that can consistently and reliably produce your product or service. Think of the production of panels as an example of something that is now moving into that *mature* stage soon to become a commodity type of product."

Ecocycle Planning *

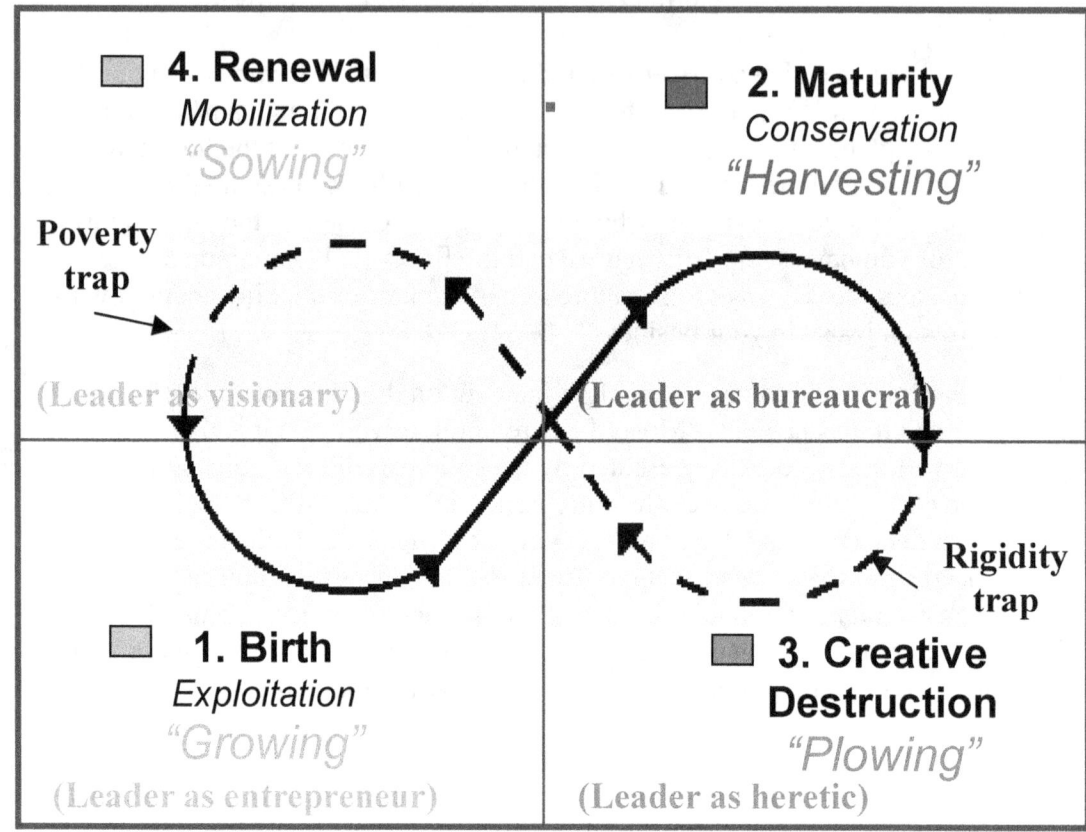

4. Renewal
Mobilization
"Sowing"

2. Maturity
Conservation
"Harvesting"

Poverty trap

(Leader as visionary)

(Leader as bureaucrat)

Rigidity trap

1. Birth
Exploitation
"Growing"

(Leader as entrepreneur)

3. Creative Destruction
"Plowing"

(Leader as heretic)

* Adapted from Hurst and Zimmerman, *From Lifecycle to Ecocycle: A New perspective on the Growth, Maturity, Destruction and Renewal of Complex Systems.*

Mike folds his arms and looks over at the line employees listening intently to Sean and thinks, *these guys don't care about this stuff! It's way over their heads anyway.* At the same moment, Vicki is watching Mike out of the corner of her eye and almost if she was reading his mind, says to herself, *they're smarter than you realize Mike.*

Sean continues, "Most people are familiar with what's needed at each part of those two stages but what we are not good at is recognizing what comes *after* and *before* each of those stages. First is the phase of *creative destruction* where we close out what needs to die, much like you need to clear space in a forest for new seedlings to flourish. Second is the phase of renewal where we seed, explore and fund new possibilities to see what new products, services, and practices have potential. Both of these phases have their own unique traps: The Rigidity trap where we won't let go of products, practices and behaviors that need to die, and the Poverty trap of not giving new ideas some space or funding to see if they have real potential."

Realizing this is a lot to digest, Sean stops. "Questions so far?"

Jonah asks, "Sean under creative destruction you use the word *heretic* as leader. Why that?"

Based on the way Jonah asked the question, Sean figures Jonah has an answer, "What do you think Jonah?"

Jonah replies, "Because you kind of need to be a heretic to say something that has been successful before and everyone is familiar with needs to be killed."

Vicki smiles at this thinking to herself, *Thank you Jonah! He is a sharp one.*

Sean smiles, "Exactly right Jonah! This is probably the hardest step in this entire process – admitting that something needs to die so that we can make room for the new. People can get very attached to their products, projects and ways of doing things, but I think we all understand that we cannot make room for new possibilities unless we take some things off our plates."

Seeing people around the table nod at this, Sean moves ahead. "Okay enough talking about models. Let's use it. What I want you to do is use the template on the next page and first *individually* identify where you see the various products, services, practices and initiatives we have going on right now in the Solon world and in particular, here at the plant and place them where you think they are in this cycle. Then we'll work in three small groups to see how we see things and ultimately as a large group…"

Monday September 11, 8:55 a.m.

The group is wrapping up its work using the Ecocycle model and Sean has written on the flipchart where the group is in agreement on a number of the major initiatives, products, etc. There is a buzz around the room as people chat about what came out of the discussion and what it might mean. Vicki gets up and heads over to the flipchart. Sean takes this as a cue that she wants the floor so he sits down.

Vicki announces, "So let's see what we're saying here. What I'm hearing, that's new anyway, is that one of the things we agree needs to die is the Earth Day event, because it's a big effort for little gain at this point, is that right?"

Ecocycle Template
Summary of 3 Groups

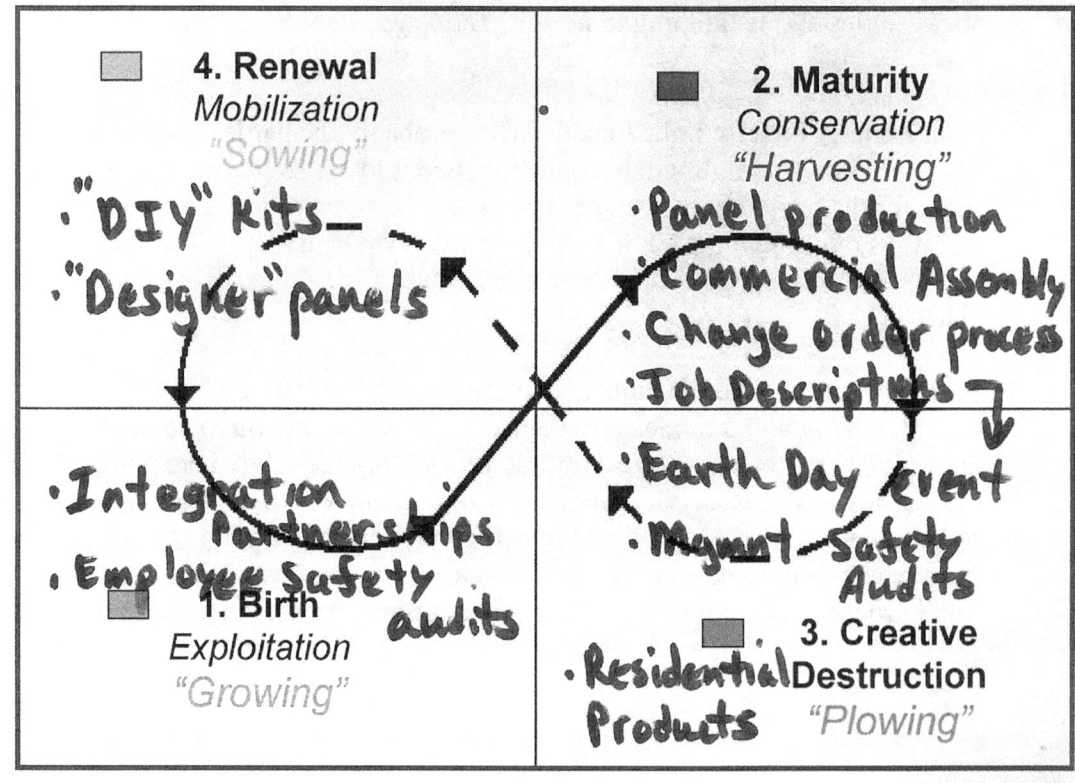

"Yes," Marcus says, "At one time it made sense and fit with our sustainable image, but it sounds like even the line folks don't see much value in it anymore."

Vicki nods, "Okay, it looks like we're saying the management GMP/safety audits don't make sense anymore either?" Vicki looks over at Steve and Ty to confirm.

Ty looks at Steve then responds, "Yeah, it always seemed to be an exercise in 'gotcha' before and now I think most everyone in the plant knows the importance, and I think we should be able to police ourselves without having to go through all the effort of an official audit."

Vicki looks Amanda's way, "Amanda…does that work for you?"

"Wow! I don't know. There may be a way to meet the OSHA requirement without going through the current process, I guess. How about I meet off-line with Steve and Ty to figure this out?" Amanda offers.

"Perfect!" says Vicki, "We've now taken two things off our plates and that was one of the main goals of this exercise. Now the last one on our Destroy list, residential products, we've already announced we're phasing out, but I'm glad to see that each of the three groups put it there, and now we have room to entertain some of the things in our Sowing/Exploring quadrant. Now, let's stop for a moment because more important than identifying specific action items right now is that we all understand how this model works. If we understand how it works, I'd like to shift gears and start looking at the ideas employees came up with in the meetings last week and see how they align with what we just did. Does that make sense?" Seeing no objections, Vicki continues, "Okay then, Sam, why don't you start. What were the better ideas that came out of your meeting?"

later that afternoon…

Vicki is in her office looking over some reports and reflecting on the morning meeting. There were some substantive things that came out of the discussions. Besides the Earth Day event and safety audits, the groups identified at least five other things that could be stopped. Vicki said she would put out a voice mail out to that effect, but also asked everyone to sit down with the people in their area and, using the Ecocycle summary they generated, walk the others through what happened. When Mike asked "why bother?", Vicki explained that it's one thing to tell everyone what we decided, but it's another to show them *how* we came to those conclusions. Vicki asked Tanya to take a picture of the summary flipchart and send it to the attendees so they can use it in their subsequent meetings. Vicki's thoughts are interrupted as Amanda pokes her head in the door.

"Hey Vicki, you got a few minutes?" Amanda asks.

Vicki laughs, "Hah! Let's see," she holds her hands up like she's juggling, "talk with Amanda or analyze these reports some more? Hmm, a tough one." She chuckles winking to Amanda and waving her to a chair. Vicki joins her at the round table. "What's going on, Amanda?"

"Well," Amanda starts, "I've been thinking about this switch from us running the audits to employees running them and I found myself, to use one of your words, 'over-engineering' things and that's when I realized I probably shouldn't be trying to figure out this by myself."

"Well…the good news is you caught yourself in the moment and recognized what you were doing!" Vicki compliments her.

"Yeah, I guess. Anyway I was thinking about that notion of 'min specs' you and Sean told us about and I thought maybe that's the way to go here, but I'm not sure how to proceed." Amanda explains.

"Well, I think your instincts are right on Amanda! Now the first thing is to get the right people in the room with us. Since we're handing it over to employees, we should have a couple line folks in this conversation. Why don't you see if Kisha can free up two of her people and have Tanya find a time when the four of us can meet. I'm in all week." Vicki offers.

"Okay, that sounds good. Should I leave it alone then until we get together?" Asks Amanda.

"For the most part yes, I would say the one thing you can think about is what are the few critical things that must happen for us to meet that OSHA requirement. Other than that, I wouldn't spend anymore time on it."

"Okay, I like that idea, less work for me!" Amanda smiles and gets up to leave.

Henry has been waiting outside Vicki's office. As Amanda leaves Henry says hello and then pokes his head in Vicki's office.

"Hi Vicki, you got a minute?" he asks.

"You mean I can't get back to my reports!?! Heaven forbid!" Vicki says kiddingly.

Henry looks confused and stops in his tracks.

"Inside joke Henry, I'm just kidding. C'mon in." She says gesturing to him to sit at the table with her.

Henry sits, than realizing the door is still open, quietly shuts it. Vicki can tell by his demeanor that something's bothering him.

Henry starts, "Vijay just stopped by my office. Seems that Mike has not taken any action on cross-training people from the different functional areas like he was supposed to. I know he hasn't gotten around to it yet, and I thought it was because of all the other stuff we have going on so I haven't brought it up with him yet. But now his people are wondering what's going on."

Vicki leans back in her chair and grimaces, "Mike, Mike, Mike, Mike, Mike…what are we going to do with you?" she exhales shaking her head. Leaning forward again she looks Henry in the eye. "Henry, this is an overdue conversation, but we need to deal with this because I'm starting to lose my patience with him, even if you're not, and that's not good."

"I know, I know," Henry pleads, "but he knows this plant and how it works better than almost anyone. It's hard to argue with his results. Our on-time delivery performance is as good as it is because of him."

Vicki can see that Henry has been struggling with this issue so she resists the urge to launch into a Mike diatribe. She takes a deep breath and exhales slowly.

"Okay Henry, you're right. I need to make sure I don't let my personal feelings toward Mike cloud my judgment as plant manager. The other thing I want to avoid is getting in the middle of a conversation that should be between the two of you. So let's think through this." Vicki pauses for a moment to collect her thoughts.

She continues, "Here's where I am and you tell me if this makes sense. I have not closed the door on Mike but it's closing quickly. There is no doubt he's a capable supervisor and can get things done, but either he does not seem to understand what we're trying to do *or* he doesn't want it and I think it's the latter. What do you think?"

"I agree – he thinks it's a waste of time and is more comfortable just telling people what to do." Henry replies.

Vicki continues, "and I can see how that might be appealing right now. We're in this experimenting phase as we rework how things are done here - someone unafraid to just take charge and make decisions looks very attractive, but that is *not* going to serve us over the long-term because it makes us too dependent on the Mike's of the world, comprendes!?!" Vicki pauses as she realizes she's letting her emotions get the best of her.

"Yes, yes, I see what you're saying," Henry says resignedly. "What do you want to do?"

"You know Henry," Vicki starts, "normally I would put the question back to you to answer, but I'm tired and I'm cranky, so I'm going to tell. I think you need to have a hard conversation with Mike on both the small issue of getting the cross-training going and on the bigger issue of whether he can truly get behind what we're trying to do here, and if not, then he should find a place more suited to his style!"

Henry is a bit taken aback. "Wow, that's a bit…

"harsh?" Vicki offers.

"yeah!" Henry exhales.

"You're right! And frankly Henry, I don't care! I've seen this pattern of behavior before from other what I call 'old school' type of supervisors. They don't really want to give up control, but they'll play along on the surface while subtly undermining things behind your back. We can't have it." Vicki finishes but keeps her gaze on Henry to let him know how serious she is.

Henry holds his hands up in defeat, "Okay! Okay!, I'll talk to him."

Friday September 15 3:45 p.m.

Activity and tensions have been running high all week. With the stopping of some practices and the beginning of others, things have been a bit on the chaotic side. No surprise to Vicki, some people are rolling with it, while others are having their struggles.

Vicki met with Amanda and a couple of Kisha's people to work on a min specs approach to employee run GMP/Safety audits. They came up with the following guidelines (min specs):

- Meet the necessary OSHA standards for conducting and reporting
- Rotate/share the burden among all line groups
- Do not impede regular production

Vicki confirmed with Amanda that as long as these conditions were met, Amanda would leave the "how" to the line folks to figure out. After the meeting, Amanda stuck around to chat with Vicki and asked her if it didn't make sense to take the same approach with the cross-training between production and assembly. Vicki agreed and said she would mention it to Henry to suggest to Mike.

Henry has had a rough week. Between ironing out some product requirements in the contract with Solar Solutions and the other initiatives going on, he is feeling a bit overwhelmed. Part of him is grateful for the activity because he has been dreading a conversation with Mike, but it's Friday and he told Vicki he would talk with Mike by the end of the week. He has called Mike on the phone and asked him to stop by to discuss something. As Mike enters Henry's office he can sense by Henry's attitude that this is not going to be a friendly chat. Mike sits gently on the chair ready to put his guard up any moment.

"Mike, there's something I want to talk to you about regarding the changes going on around here." Henry starts off somberly.

Mike feels his guard going up quickly. "What's the problem?" he asks a bit defensively.

"Mike you have always been one of our most conscientious workers so I'm not sure what to make of this. I'm sure it was just an oversight." Henry offers.

Mike, sensing that Henry is being evasive, says, "What is it Henry? Just say it!"

Henry is clearly not comfortable with this conversation. "We're wondering why you haven't made any movement on the cross-raining, that was supposed to have started a couple months ago." Henry says accusingly.

"Whoa, whoa!" Mike responds "who says I'm not working on it. I've *been* working on it. I'm still thinking it through."

Henry retorts, "Yes, but that's just it Mike, we're not sure you should be figuring this all out by yourself, and that leads to the larger issue, of whether you are truly behind this employee engagement effort."

"Now hold on a minute Henry! First, who is this 'we' you keep referring to? Is this you speaking or Vicki?" Mike replies hotly.

Henry is embarrassed to be called out on speaking for people not in the room. "Well, it's both of us, but right now it's me. We..I don't want to lose a good manager..." Henry starts.

Mike sits back in his chair gripping the armrests, "Whoa, are you telling me I'm on notice!?!" Mike exclaims.

Henry starts to backpedal. "No! No!, that's not it at all. We..I just want to know what's going on?"

"There's nothing going on Henry. C'mon man, you and I have been working together now for three years. Look at what she's got going on here! We got employees running safety audits, they're questioning Marcus's purchasing decisions, Vijay is inviting competing Integrators to sit down together! This is crazy! C'mon, you see the havoc it's causing." Mike exclaims.

Henry has decided the reasonable approach is not going to work, so he shifts into a more formal, authoritarian manner. "Mike, that may be true to some degree, but I don't think you're taking the appropriate attitude here. I think we need to give these things some time, and I need you to involve your people more in moving the cross-training forward. For now, let's just focus on that and we can revisit the other issue later. I'm sorry I need to be this way, but this is what we're doing!" Henry says adamantly.

Mike is gripping the armrests even harder and has to stop himself from blurting something that will only get him into more trouble. "Fine, I'll get on it Monday." He says in a huff.

Henry trying to salvage something from the conversation, "Good! I appreciate your help." He says with a forced smile.

Mike slips out of Henry's office fuming, while Henry puts his head in his hand thinking, *Well, that certainly good have gone better.*

After a few minutes, Henry heads down to Vicki's office to talk with her only to find out from Tanya that Vicki got a last minute call from Rolf that he was in town and wanted to have a dinner meeting. Henry's shoulders slump at this news and he mopes back to his office where he sends off an e-mail to Vicki saying,

> *Vicki, can we meet before the staff meeting Monday? – had my talk with Mike – could have gone better.*
>
> *Henry*

Monday, September 18, 7:00 a.m.

Vicki is meeting with Henry in her office. They had conversed over the weekend via e-mail and agreed to get together at 7:00. Henry brooded all weekend over his encounter with Mike and is sitting at the table with Vicki not looking happy.

"Okay Henry, your cryptic message had me wondering all weekend. What happened?" Vicki asks.

"Sorry, I didn't mean to be so vague. I guess it went okay. He agreed to get going on the cross-training" Henry starts.

"Well that's good," Vicki acknowledges, "but I'm looking at you Henry and you don't seem convinced."

"Well, it did get pretty heated, and I think I got a little defensive." Henry replies.

Vicki stays quiet sensing he has more to say.

"You know, he brought up some good points Vicki. We do have a lot of stuff going on and it's a little crazy right now." Henry argues.

"Yes, you're right Henry. It is a bit crazy right now, and I know that can be frustrating for folks, but I've learned that's a part of any change process. There's always a period of chaos as people are trying out new ways to find the best fit. I've come to see it as a natural, albeit scary, part of the process." Vicki empathizes.

Henry exhales some at hearing this. "Yeah, I guess, but how do we know this is going to work out. Will Rolf appreciate what we're trying to do here?" Henry asks with concern.

"Wow, Henry. The honest answer is I don't know. I only know that whenever I have turned to employees in the other places I have worked, and sincerely engaged them in helping me figure out how to improve things, they have always stepped up. Will they do it this time? I think we're already seeing evidence they *will*. Will Rolf be patient with us on seeing the fruits of this? That I can't answer. I can only say that *I think* this is worth doing, even if Rolf doesn't see the value in it. I know that's risky, but it's what I believe. The question is Henry, do *you* think it's worth doing?" Vicki keeps her eyes on Henry with an inquiring, but friendly gaze.

Henry pauses for a moment "Yes, I do, but I'm still not sure what we should do about Mike."

"Do you think you need to have a follow-up talk with him? It sounds like it didn't end well." Vicki asks.

Henry counters, "No, at least not right away. Mike and I have worked together long enough that we both know we need to just cool off for a bit and I think it will blow over."

"Okay we can let it go for now, but I think we need to keep an eye on him. Based on what you told me, I'm still not sure he's going to come around." Vicki warns.

"Yeah, unfortunately, I think you're right." Henry concludes.

at the staff meeting a little later…

The team has gone over the order's for the week and other immediate issues. It did not go unnoticed by Vicki and Henry that Mike has been a little quieter and more abrupt in his comments than normal.

"Okay, let's move to 'ongoing initiatives' on the agenda. Henry, you've been working with Vijay on the labeling meeting. Everything coming together?" Vicki asks.

Henry hands out a piece of paper to everyone while responding. "Yes, as you can see we've invited four other Integrators in the region and Solar Consulting and New Energy Options each want to attend. The other two are still checking their schedules, but indicated they would like to join."

Vicki replies, "Great, make sure you check with Ryan on how many people he's bringing from corporate, to make sure we have enough room. Alright, next…Mike - cross-training between production and assembly – where are we?" Vicki of course, knows the answer but does not want Mike to escape the consequences of his inaction. Peer pressure, she has learned, is a beautiful thing.

"I'm going to meet with my supervisors today and start planning it." Mike says curtly.

"Great!" Vicki replies, "But I want to have some line folks in on that conversation, and I think the min specs approach we took with the audits might be the way to go here. What do you think Amanda?" Vicki looks Amanda's way.

"Yes. I think it could work well there." Amanda confirms.

Mike feels the groups' eyes on him and is not ready to back off yet. "Well, I don't know that I understand this min specs idea well enough to implement it in our area." He counters.

"No problem," Vicki says smiling, "I think Amanda would be more than happy to help. Amanda?" She looks at Amanda and smiles.

"Sure, it's not that complicated. Mike, how about we get together for a couple minutes after the meeting?" Amanda offers.

Mike realizing he is cornered now relents, "Okay, sure."

"Great! Next item – Jonah – where are we with this social networking software you've been playing with?" Vicki asks.

Sheepishly Jonah replies "Yeah, I don't think we can make much use of it."

"Why's that Jonah?" Vicki probes.

"Well, we just don't have the scale of people and business lines to take advantage of it." Jonah begins. "The software is good for unearthing the natural networks inside any organization to uncover who is really respected and sought after inside an organization. If we were really big with lots of plants and people scattered around the country, that data could prove useful, but since we're so small, I don't think we can make much use of it." Jonah's voice trails off.

"Well, at least it didn't cost us anything." Marcus offers.

"Well, it does cost some time and effort to explore these things," Vicki starts, "but I don't want us to lose sight of the fact that we need to figure out a way to do this kind of experimenting. Even though this didn't pan out, you never know what we might stumble upon that will. What I'm trying to say Jonah, is don't let the fact that this experiment didn't pan out discourage you." Seeing a nod and a half smile from Jonah, Vicki realizes he got the message.

"I have an idea." Tanya says.

Everyone stops in their tracks and looks at Tanya. Up to this point in the management team meetings, she has only spoken when asked something directly.

"I've submitted some designs on Shirtworld.com where they let people vote on the T-shirt designs and based on what people choose, they make those T-shirts." Tanya stops for a moment because she's not sure they want to hear her idea.

"And so…" Vicki prompts her.

Tanya continues, "and so, I was thinking why don't we do something like that to get people interested in our designer panel idea?"

Jonah looks at Tanya with surprise "You mean ask people to submit their own designs for panels?"

"Or at least poll them for their thoughts on the idea" Vicki adds looking at Jonah. She continues, "Tanya, I think you may have something there! Jonah, what do you think?"

"I think, at a minimum, it can't hurt to poll previous customers and potential customers for their thoughts." Jonah begins, "We may even get some people from the design world interested in some kind of contest – and we can let customers vote on their favorites – as long as the designers stay within certain boundaries we have to build in."

Jonah realizes he is off on his own rapid thought stream and stops himself. He looks over at Tanya and smiles. "Tanya, where've you been hiding!" he winks at her. Tanya blushes and smiles.

Vicki is pleased both at Tanya taking a risk and in Jonah's encouragement of that.

"Thanks Tanya" she smiles, "and I hope you always feel welcome to share an idea."

Looking back at the group, "Okay, where are we…"

"Rules" - Part 2

When going down the path of fuller engagement, expect a fair amount of "two steps forward, one step back." You are trying to change "parent to child" patterns of behavior between management and employees that have often been in place for years. Both sides are used to, and to a certain degree, comfortable in their roles: management as parent and employee as child. This is why the prevailing pattern in most organizations is that management organizes the work and employees wait to be told. Even when management makes a good faith effort to reach out and engage more, employees first reaction may be lukewarm. This could be due to:

a) It's unusual (not the norm)
b) They are suspicious (what are they *really* after?)
c) They are fearful of being accountable ("*I don't want to step up, let me remain innocent!*")

Regardless of the reason, expect fits and starts. Also, in the early stages of engaging others more purposefully, expect that the ideas you get may be all over the board in terms of quality. This is usually due to the employee's lack of understanding of the overall business and the level and amount of information available to them, and *not* a function of their intelligence. It's important for leaders to remember this because the initial ideas they get may not seem well thought out and it will provide ammunition for the "non-believers" to say, "See, I told you this 'engagement stuff' was a waste of time!"

This leads us to the next rule of engagement for leaders. When gathering employees and asking for their ideas on sustaining and improving the business, remember that the **quality of the interaction is more important than the quality of the ideas**. Another way of saying it is that *how* you engage employees in that conversation, is more important than what specific ideas or results comes out of it. The first few times getting a group together and asking for their thoughts, you may be better served lowering your expectations. Again, remember that they enter that conversation dealing with the a,b,c baggage noted above. Don't be surprised if both the quality and boldness is lacking in the beginning; the quality will be there eventually. What's not shown in our Solon story is that for each good idea people come up with, e.g. "having employees organize and run the audits," there were probably five others, at least, that were less than good. NOTE: At the same time, you should also brace yourself for rather *bold* ideas. My experience is that line folks are often more willing to be bold in rethinking things because they have less to lose in changing the status quo.

Regardless of what you initially get in the way of ideas and input, the key to remember is the only sustainable path is to focus on *good process*. The visual below may help as a reminder as to what leaders want to remember about handling these discussions.

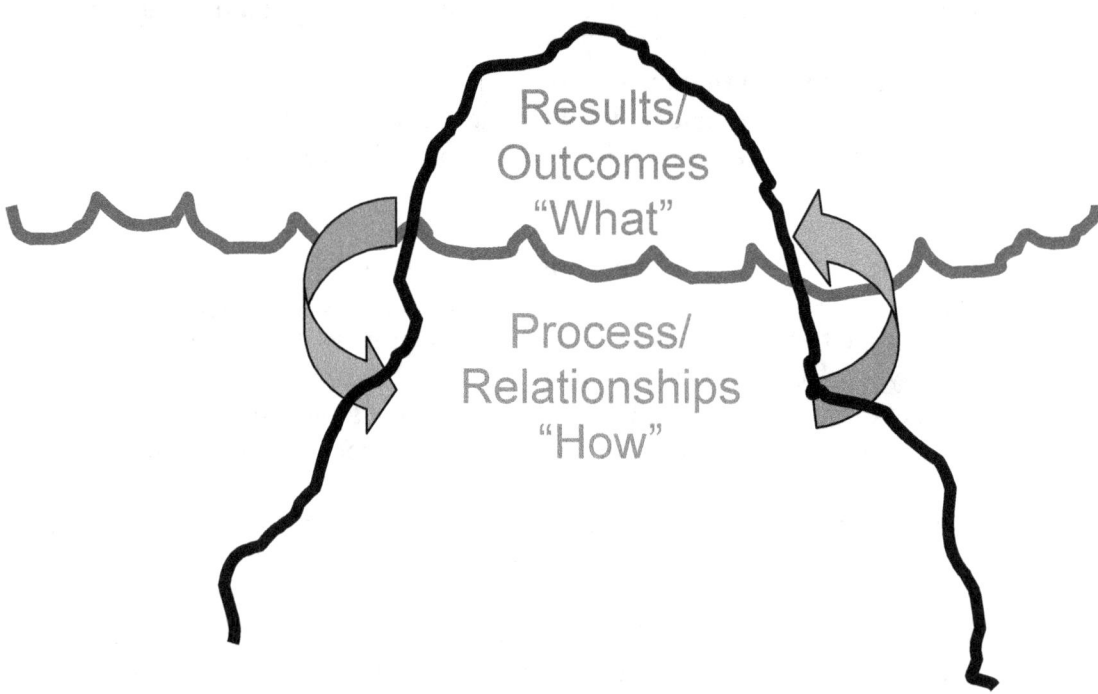

Like the part of the iceberg above the waterline, leaders all too often focus just on "what" actionable thing or quality ideas come out of these discussions and all too often ignore the importance of "how" they handled the conversation. If you want to eventually get to a place where employees feel comfortable stepping up to share their best thinking, focus on good *process*.

The other thing leaders must prepare for is to help employees with questions of *faith* as they step up to share more ownership of the whole. By faith, I am not talking about religious faith, but the faith being called for in response to the following type of questions you may get from employees:

1. If we join you in improving the business, does that assure us future employment?
2. How do we know upper management will not pull the plug on this?
3. If we stay with this, will you be there for us later?
4. Will upper management continue to support this effort?
5. Will they be patient with our mistakes?
6. If there's a change in management or drop in the market, will we stick with this?
7. After all you've told us, is it worth it? Why should I stick my neck out?

Now you may be saying that employees don't typically voice these kinds of questions aloud, but I think we know from experience these questions are there whether voiced or not. The question becomes how will you respond when posed one of these questions of faith? This leads to our next rule of engagement for leaders, **questions of "faith" must be answered personally**. What I mean is, don't patronize, don't sell, don't cajole, don't spin, don't try to inspire. No speaking on behalf of or for others. No "*we* feel/think" responses. What you can do is answer for yourself. In italics below are some responses to the questions above, that I would love to hear leaders use more often:

1. *I can't guarantee that.* (If we join you in improving the business, does that assure us future employment?)
2. *That could happen, I won't deny it.* (How do we know upper management will not pull the plug on this?)
3. *I can only tell you that I will do everything in my power to keep you informed.* (If we stay with this, will you be there for us later?)
4. *I don't know.* (Will upper management continue to support this effort?)
5. *I don't know.* (Will they be patient with our mistakes?)
6. *I don't know.* (If there's a change in management or a big drop in revenue, will we still stick with this?)
7. *I can't answer that for you. I can only tell you that I believe it's worth it.* (After all you've told us, is it worth it? Why should I stick my neck out?)

In our Solon story we start to see Henry's faith flag when he asks Vicki (p. 89) if "Rolf appreciates what we're trying to do here?" Notice that Vicki in her response does not try to reassure or placate Henry. Instead, she gives an honest answer, "I don't know", and goes on to say that she believes it's worth doing. This is what we mean by a *personal* response to questions of faith.

Rules of Engagement

1. Admit to your limitations in controlling things.
2. Bring the really tough questions directly to employees AND stop organizing their efforts.
3. Clarify the What and Why but stay out of the How.
4. Take a "min specs" approach when defining boundaries around how people can go about doing their work.
5. **The quality of interaction is more important than the quality of ideas.**
6. **Questions of "faith" must be answered personally.**

Part 3:

Making Conscious Choices

"Good questions work on us, we don't work on them. They are not a project to be completed but a doorway opening onto a greater depth of understanding, action that will take us into being more fully alive. Acting on what matters is, ultimately, a political stance, one whereby we declare we are accountable for the world around us and we are willing to pursue what we define as important, independent of whether it is in demand, or has market value."

~ Peter Block, *The Answer to How Is Yes*

Friday, December 1, 7:10 p.m.

The last three months have been a whirlwind. Productivity at the plant is up 8% overall as compared to last quarter. Not bad, but not the 10-15% Vicki was shooting for. Fall scheduling went smoothly. Henry prodded Mike to take a min specs approach to that as well and leave it to his four supervisors and their direct reports to figure out. Because of the cross-training that is now almost complete, they are able to be more flexible with scheduling. Employees are much happier being able to negotiate with each other rather than having to get management approval. Mike was not happy with the decision, but can't argue with the results.

Meetings with employees to walk through the results of the Ecocycle Planning results were a mixed bag. Within each group that gathered, some employees took a keen interest in the discussion; while some just took up seats. This did not surprise Vicki and she reminded her management team that, it may take a while for some employees to come around and a few may never step up, but it's worth it if just for the 40%-60% or so that do.

The meeting with the Integrators and the UL representative was also a mixed bag. The new labeling guidelines are going to produce more snags than Vijay and Henry anticipated, but they were able to clarify some requirements with the UL person ahead of time that will help them be more proactive. Having some Integrators there helped from the standpoint that it gave all the Solon attendees more insight into what's going on in the Integrator world. The VP of sales for Sun Works appreciated being invited and Ryan Connelly from Solon's Corporate Sales said this might help us with the sale of a long-term contract with them.

At the end of October, employees piloted the first new GMP/Safety audit process, and Amanda was happy to report that overall it went very well. There are a few bugs to work out, but employees responded much better to being challenged by a *peer* to keep up to standards. Vicki had a chuckle at this news and reminded Amanda that "peer pressure is a beautiful thing, no?"

Except for Mike, the management team is starting to be more conscious of making efforts to engage employees more in questions of *what* and *why* and leaving the *how* up to them. There have been some hiccups here and there, but overall, employees have responded positively to the new approach. A few even had to be pulled in a bit as their enthusiasm for showing initiative got a little out of hand. Jonah seems to show a real knack for being able to give people a clear sense of the boundaries they need to stay in as they experiment. Mike, on the other hand, has come along reluctantly. Henry is finally starting to lose patience with Mike. He is not looking forward to that conversation, but is starting to realize that it seems inevitable.

At this moment, Vicki is in her car on her way back from a meeting in San Francisco with Rolf. Rolf had called this morning to say he was flying up for some meetings at Solon Corporate and had some big news for Vicki and big news it was. She is relaying the news over the phone to her husband George.

"Yes! Can you believe it!?! The Governor of New Jersey wants to have us operating in some form by the end of this year, so he can cite it as an accomplishment going into the election year." Vicki exclaims.

"But you can't get something up and running in one month, can you?" George replies.

"That's what I told Rolf, but he said we don't need to be fully operational, just be hiring and have a site identified the governor can point to. It's a challenge, but I think it's doable. Listen honey, I'll tell you more when I get home. I want to call Henry and give him the news. I should be home in an hour. Love you! By" Vicki concludes.

Vicki hangs up with George and dials Henry's cell only to get his voice mail. She leaves a message.

"Henry, it's me. Listen, call me on my cell as soon as you get this. I want to fill you in on my meeting with Rolf."

An hour later Vicki heard back from Henry and filled him in on the news. Henry was shocked to hear how quickly things would need to happen and what this would mean for him and his family. Mostly he kept saying "wow" and tried to match Vicki's enthusiasm for the news. Vicki asked that they both think about the implications of this and meet 7:00 a.m. Monday to discuss plans.

Monday December 4, 7:00 a.m.

Vicki is in her office making some notes on the whiteboard. Her energy is up and she's a little more anxious than normal as she spent the weekend thinking through what all this means and how to respond. When Henry comes in she is so caught up in her thoughts, she does not notice his grim demeanor.

"Hey Henry, have a seat" she says staying at the whiteboard and continuing to jot down some notes. Looking at the whiteboard she points to an agenda saying quickly, "I was thinking we can start with how soon we can get you out there to check out the site and who to take along. Then we can discuss..."

"Uh, Vicki, hold on a second" Henry interrupts.

Vicki stops and looks fully at Henry for the first time and sees he's looking troubled. "What is it Henry?"

"We don't want to go." He says solemnly.

"What do you mean you don't want to go!" Vicki says with some alarm creeping into her voice.

"To Jersey. We discussed it all weekend and decided we like it here and don't want to move." Henry says looking down.

Vicki is not ready to give in, "Look if it's because of the school year, we can probably set you up with temporary housing and then you can bring the family out next summer. Henry, I need you on this!"

Vicki is blatantly putting on the full court press now. She wants Henry to take the new role.

Henry is resolute. "It's not the school year Vicki. We realized after many conversations that we don't want to move. I know that might limit my options here, but that's where we are."

Vicki's shoulders slump as she realizes Henry is not budging.

"Damn, Henry, this is not the way I saw this meeting going!" Vicki exclaims throwing her head back in frustration.. She sits down and is quiet for a moment.

"No changing your mind on this huh?" she asks.

"No, I'm sorry Vicki." He says feeling guilty now.

"No, don't be sorry. Yes, I'm angry, but I'm glad you stuck to your guns Henry. George and I had our own conversations about what all this means and whether we really want it also." She explains.

Vicki is lost in her own thoughts for a minute, before she perks up a bit. "Okay then. Henry, we still need to figure out what the hell we're going to do! I told Rolf I'd have a plan to him by Friday so help me figure this out. And by the way, I don't want this news to deter us from dealing with the Mike situation. We need to stay on top of that...."

Friday December 8, 9:00 a.m.

The next few days were a flurry of activity. Vicki called an emergency all-hands meeting on Tuesday to announce the news about the new plant and told everyone she would provide more details on Friday. She was happy to see that while there was some increase in gossip and speculation, for the most part people stayed focused and seemed content to wait until Friday for the details. She was also relieved to see that Henry sat down with Mike and had a hard conversation with him about his behavior. Henry indicated that he thought it went very well, and that Mike was already looking at other options and realized it was probably best if he found something else.

Everyone is gathered on the factory floor for the all-hands meeting. People are seated theater-style facing the front. Vicki and Sean are sitting up front side by side facing the group. They are chatting quietly. Sitting in scattered seats amongst the line employees is the rest of the management team, except for Mike who is conspicuously absent.

Vicki gets up and announces, "Okay everybody, let's get started. I know you've been waiting to hear more details about the new facility, and I appreciate your patience this past week! Sean is with us again because I wanted him to help us figure out how we are going to respond to this challenge. Sean and I thought the Open Space process might be an effective way to engage all of you in helping us figure this out. So, after I give you the particulars about what has been decided and why, and some of the boundaries we have to work within, I'm going to hand it over to Sean to take us through the process."

Vicki pauses for a moment to make sure she has everyone's attention.

"Now some of you may be wondering why Mike is not here. I don't think it's a surprise to anyone to say that Mike was having difficulty adjusting to the way we wanted management and line personnel to interact here going forward. Mike has been a loyal Solon employee and we wish him well. After chatting with him, he informed us that he found a position with Scott Hasting's contract manufacturing company and we wish him luck with that. He will be around for another couple weeks to tie up loose ends so we encourage everyone to wish Mike well when you get a chance."

This generates a certain amount of buzz as Vicki expected so she stops for a moment to let that run it's course.

Vicki continues, "Now the next thing has to do with management at the New Jersey facility. I'm sure most of you could figure out that Henry was being readied to take on that role. In searching his heart Henry came to the conclusion that he didn't want to disrupt his family's life to that degree. I want to commend Henry publicly for sticking to his principles and working with me to find a solution that I think works for him and the business. So, Henry will be staying put."

She looks at Henry who is sitting in the front row and nods and Henry nods back.

Vicki continues, "I am choosing to be candid and transparent with you about the conversations and issues that go into these discussions and decisions because a) I think you can handle it and b) I'm guessing you wrestle with the same kinds of things yourselves so you can appreciate the situation Henry was facing. Now, lucky for us, we have someone who *is* qualified and is from the New Jersey area originally so it is a win/win for this person because they get a challenging work opportunity and move back closer to home. Please join me in congratulating *Jonah* as the new plant manager for the New Jersey facility."

Vicki gestures toward Jonah to stand. After gasps of surprise, people start clapping and whistling for Jonah. He stands up and waves and smiles feeling a bit embarrassed by the attention. Jonah has always been one of the more popular managers at the facility, and its evident as people stand and clap for him while looking at each other nodding.

After people sit again and the buzz quiets down, Vicki resumes, "Jonah will be back and forth between the 2 facilities quite a bit over the next few weeks so you will have plenty of chances to catch up with him. "

"Now, the last bit of, I guess, big news. Henry's soul searching about what is best for him and his family forced me to do the same. I have enjoyed working with all of you this past year. I especially loved how each time the management team came to you with tough questions, you have not shied away from addressing them."

People in the crowd start looking at each other and wondering where Vicki is going with this.

She continues, "The situation now is that Henry is more than ready to lead this plant and I am ready to do what I love which is show companies how management and employees can better work together. So, effective January 1, Henry will be the plant manager here and I will be joining Sean's consulting practice."

More gasps and stunned faces at this news. Before people can respond, Vicki plows ahead. "Now I have the utmost faith in Henry and part of the deal I negotiated with the Nu Energies Management is that I would spend the next 6 months helping Jonah get the New Jersey facility up and running and help Henry with his transition. So, you haven't seen the last of me. I'll be in and out for the next six months at least." Vicki says smiling.

Sensing that people need some time to digest all this, Vicki calls a break and asks everyone to reconvene in ten minutes. As people get up to break off into informal discussions, Vicki seeks Henry out.

"It's all yours now Henry!" she says reaching out to shake his hand. "I think you should kick off the Open Space session instead of me, agree?"

"Yeah, I guess you're right." Henry replies. He is quiet for a moment as he looks over the various employee groups chatting in small groups energetically about the news.

"I guess there's no going back is there Vicki?" He says continuing to watch the groups chat away.

"What do you mean?" Vicki replies.

"I mean in terms of involving people going forward. I get the feeling that once they get a taste of being more fully engaged, they don't want to go back."

Vicki laughs then smiles at Henry, "You're right about that Henry. There's no going back for these folks, so get ready for an adventure!"

THE END

Final Thoughts

I have been purposely brief in my summaries after each chapter. When you decide to truly partner with others inside your organization and fully bring them into the decision-making process, you create conditions where there are *more* unknowns for you as management, not less. Where before you may have decided things on your own and brought that to the group, you will now find yourself entering conversations wondering "will they see things the same way I do and come to the same conclusions about what to do?" The *partnering* route does not lend itself to easy formulas or recipes. Trying to go into a meeting with a plan to bring the group to a predetermined answer almost always backfires and as soon as you start thinking that way, you're back in the patriarchy mindset. While you may get a nod and pseudo agreement in the meeting, people will dig their heels in later no matter how right you feel the solution may be. People ultimately resist coercion no matter how well-intended. For these reasons, I avoided getting into lengthy scripts and process steps to engagement and stayed, instead, at the level of principles.

Certainly the culture change Vicki was going for would take longer than a year. In most cases, someone in Vicki's position would need to give it at least 1 and ½ to 3 years to see sustainable change. I took some literary license in order to keep the story brief and tie things up quickly. In the end, the best approach for any leader is to step up and offer an idea of what could be and why you feel it's important. If others agree with you on those two points, you're halfway home. The last step is to let them help you figure out how.

Good Luck!
Rich McLaughlin

Author's Note

If I did not represent players in the solar panel manufacturing industry accurately, I apologize. They just provided a convenient and topical industry to base the story in. If I represented it at all well, it is mostly due to luck, but I do want to thank Pam Frank, Director of Business Development for Sunfarm Network, for her insights as an industry insider.

I would also like to thank the following people for their help and support: Carolyn Henning, Lisa Gilbert, and Andy DiFelice for their encouragement; Kathy McHugh for her editorial expertise; and my wife, Ann-Marie McHugh for her storytelling expertise and support!

Many people have influenced my thinking around the issue of employee engagement and how to organize adults to accomplish something, but the two most prominent have been Peter Block and Meg Wheatley. Peter is the best I've come across at capturing the limits of the patriarchy model of management that seems to be the predominate approach in so many organizations. Meg offers wonderful and simple alternatives for how we might rethink the way we organize to get things done. Anything by these two author's would be worth picking up but if I were to recommend one, I would go with Peter's, *Community: The Structure Of Belonging*, and Meg's, *Finding Our Way: Leadership for an Uncertain Time.*

Glossary

Cloud Computing: A way of taking advantage of computing power without investing in the hardware infrastructure yourself. Users pay a fee to a third party provider to access applications via the web thereby cutting down on their capital infrastructure costs.

Complexity Science: a term for how to study and understand complex systems (e.g., human societies, the brain) where many interdependent and independent agents cannot be controlled or defined using linear approaches. Instead of looking at individual components in a system and breaking them down via reduction, complexity science looks at *the relationship between* entities in a system as the way to understand the nature of the system.

Crowdsourcing: A term for tapping into large numbers of people via the internet to help you do everything from design a product, to finding funding for an idea to getting feedback on a product or service and/or to solving technical problems.

Leadership Assimilation: A two to four hour process designed to help accelerate trust and relationship-building between a new leader and his/her team. A series of categories are posed to the team to generate questions under while the leader is out of the room, then the leader, working with a facilitator comes into the room and engages the team by candidly answering the questions.

"Min Specs": an approach for guiding behavior in any complex system, "min specs" is short for minimum specifications. The idea is that in complex systems, overly detailed procedures and rules often become counter-productive.

A better approach is to specify a minimum set of guidelines for behavior that allows people operating in that complex system the ability to adjust their approach based on local conditions while still holding true to the overall "min specs."

Open Space Technology: A large group meeting process originally designed by Harrison Owen (*Open Space technology: A User's Guide* - see next page) that invites more engagement and ownership by attendees because they are allowed to shape the agenda and convene their own breakout discussions.

Skunkworks: a term used to describe low profile projects being conducted in an organization "under the radar" and undisturbed to allow for the creative process to better emerge.

References

1   Lee Ozley and Rich Teerlink, *More than a Motorcycle: The Harley-Davidson Story* (Harvard College, 2000) One of the best books   I've read that captures how change really unfolds when you involve everyone.

11   Neil Snyder, et.al., *Vision,Values and Courage: Leadership for Quality Management* (Free Press, 1993)

54   Harrison Owen, *Open Space Technology: A User's Guide* (Berrett-Koehler, 1997)

60   Kevin Kelly, *Out of Control: The New Biology of Machines, Social Systems and the Economic World* (Basic Books, 1995)

69   Brenda Zimmerman and David Hurst, *From Life Cycle to Ecocycle: A New Perspective on the Growth, Maturity, Destruction and Renewal of Complex Systems* (Journal of Management Inquiry, V 3, No. 4)

88   Peter Block, *The Answer to How Is Yes! Acting on What Matters* (Berrett-Koehler, 2003)

Tools

These are a few tools leaders can use to start conversations that engage employees in paying more attention to the "whole" and for promoting more initiative and self-organization.

Page

High Performance Work Systems Audit.......... 113
This is a tool to provoke conversation around how to make a more robust, engaging and effective work environment. It is a very challenging standard to achieve and can only be reached by involving everyone in the organization.

Conditions for Self-Organization 114
Words of wisdom from Meg Wheatley on the "min specs" needed to promote self-organization. You can create your own questions around the three conditions to start a conversation around the degree to which you are allowing self-organization to occur in your team/department/organization.

Employee Manifesto................................. 115
A challenge by Peter Block to all employees on how they might rethink their role and responsibility in shaping the future of the organization and their own experience within it. Consider handing it out and asking people to think of it a description of a future state of what the organization *could be* someday.

Engaging Conversations.................................. 116
An expansion of the model first introduced on page 34. This version has specific language leaders could use when engaging others in completing a task/project.

High Performance Work Systems - Audit

** Less Healthy/Robust
Hard to Sustain **

** More Healthy/Robust
Easier to Sustain **

◄ ─ ─ ─ ─ ─ ─ ─ ─ ─ ─ ─ ─ ─ ─ ─ ─ ─ ─ ►

Focus

Many people don't understand what we're trying to accomplish as a business.	1 2 3 4 5	Everyone understands at a fundamental level what we're trying to do and why it's important.
Many people don't understand how what they do supports our purpose.	1 2 3 4 5	People understand how what they do helps the business.

Information

Information (budgets, results, cash flow, etc.) is difficult to access and tightly controlled/portioned out.	1 2 3 4 5	Information is easy to access; no restrictions; flows where it needs to go; no censoring/controlling.

Freedom

Many tightly drawn, specialized jobs→ many handoffs.	1 2 3 4 5	Jobs broadly drawn → less handoffs; More people working on "wholes."
Many approvals needed for action; micromanaging others (prescribing).	1 2 3 4 5	Empowered with info.; trusting others to self-organize (describing).
Inflexible policies/procedures; "Do it *this* way, *all* the time."	1 2 3 4 5	Broad boundaries and principles to flex within; "Find your *own* way that works *for now*."
Access to others in the company is not easy; often hindered/questioned.	1 2 3 4 5	Networking/initiating direct communication is encouraged.

Diversity

Going along; complying with Mgmnt./ playing it safe is the norm.	1 2 3 4 5	Challenging unsound ideas and misalignment/Questioning status quo is the norm.
Tendency to recruit and promote people who maintain the status quo.	1 2 3 4 5	Tendency to hire for diversity of thinking/outspoken people.

Exploration

Non-traditional thinking/approaches discouraged.	1 2 3 4 5	Constructive dialogue and disagreement encouraged.
Force of personality/hierarchy/politics drives decisions.	1 2 3 4 5	The power of ideas and their viability drives decisions.

Meaning

People are given work that is not meaningful → requires extrinsic motivators that need constant maintenance.	1 2 3 4 5	People given work that is meaningful; Intrinsic motivation is high.

<u>Conditions for Self-Organization *</u>

• Clear Purpose/Identity/Goal

All organisms have a sense of identity from which there actions flow. These same organisms are constantly exploring who they are and their potential in their quest to live out their intentions. The effectiveness and development of any organism in large part depends on to what degree it understands its identity and is able to take actions that support its main purpose.

> *(Look back at any catastrophe that hits a community and you can see self-organization in action. In the aftermath of the twin towers collapsing on 9/11, self-organizing efforts sprung up all over simply driven by a clear goal "save lives")*

• Free Flow Of Information

Organisms function best when there is a free flow of information throughout their systems. Delays, approvals and filtering of information as it goes through the system tends to inhibit the effectiveness of the system because agents within the system are acting without all the available feedback/data. In self-organizing systems, information tends to go directly to the people who can make the *best* and *most immediate* use of it in their efforts to live out their purpose.

> *(This and the next condition are not required for self-organizing but effect a group's **ability** to self-organize. Going back to the WTC tragedy again, there was plenty of evidence of breakdowns that occurred between the fire and police departments due to the lack of a free flow of info. In this case, mostly due to radios that didn't communicate with each other.)*

• Freedom To Interact/Connect/Build Relationships

In natural, organic systems, agents within that system are free to interact and mingle (at any given moment) with whomever they deem necessary for the organization to live out its purpose. Asking for permission, observing protocol, boundaries, silos, etc. are behaviors that do not exist in these types of systems. As agents (e.g., employees) within a system get feedback from their interaction with the external world (customers), they are free to immediately assemble the appropriate resources to respond to that feedback.

> *(Once you have a team self-organizing around a worthy effort, the best response sometimes is to "get out of the way".)*

---

* Meg Wheatley is a former Harvard and Brigham Young University professor who has written extensively on the application of "new" science models to organizations. Specifically, she has looked at what we can learn from watching self-organizing systems in nature "go about their business."

EMPLOYEE MANIFESTO - By Peter Block

"In our efforts to create accountable, high-performing and satisfying workplaces, we most often think that if the management would change, the institution would change. We persistently want our bosses to be our mentors; we want them to take responsibility for our development. We get upset when they do not act with integrity, or work well together, articulate a clear vision, or are powerful advocates for our unit with those even higher in the institution. Here are some wishes of myself and other employees that would balance the equation and support the transformation many of us seek."

1. Care for the success and well being of the whole institution regardless of how it is managed. Stop thinking the organization has to earn our loyalty. Commit to its purpose and its customers even if things are not perfect.

2. Mentor ourselves. Find our own teachers and support. Don't expect it from the boss or from Human Resources. Be willing to pay for our own learning, recruit our own coaches, plan our own continuing education. Stop thinking the organization is responsible for our development.

3. View our boss as a struggling human being, no more able to walk their talk than we are able to walk ours.

4. Learn how to run this business. Become economically literate. Know the budget-cost-revenue connection of everything we touch. Learn as many jobs as possible. Figure out what clients and customers want and how to give it to them.

5. Be accountable for the success of our peers. Decide to support their learning and focus on their strengths, rather than be disappointed in their shortcomings. Be their mentor; see their weaknesses as an opportunity for us to learn forgiveness and tolerance. And if we get in battle with them over territory or budget, give it away.

6. Accept the unpredictability of the situation we are in. The future of the organization is a mystery and who knows how long these conditions will exist. Stop asking where we are headed. Today is where we are headed and that is enough.

7. Forget our ambition to get "ahead." Ahead of whom? Why not stop competing with those around us. The only hope we have for more prosperity is if the institution really grows. Besides, if we do get promoted, who is to say we will be any happier? My observation is that the higher you go in the organization, the more depressed you become.

8. View meetings and conversations as an investment in relationships. Value a human relationship over an electronic one.

9. Deliver on our promises and stop focusing on the actions of others. The clarity and integrity of our actions will change the world. Stop thinking and talking about the behavior of others. Let go of disappointment in them and how they were too little and too late. Maybe they had something more important to do than meet our requirements. Similarly, no one else is going to change. They are good the way they are.

10. If change is going to happen, it will be us. Ghandi said that if blood be shed let it be ours. We need to blink first. Shift our own thinking and do it for our own sake, not as a hidden bargain designed to control the actions of others.

11. Accept that most important human problems have no permanent solution. No new policy, structure, legislation or management declaration is going to fix much. Justice and progress will always happen locally, on our watch, in our unit, only as a result of our actions with those in the immediate vicinity.

12. Stop asking "how?" We now have all the skills, the methods, the tools, the capacity and the freedom to do whatever is required. All that is needed is the will and courage to choose and to move on. And to endure the uncontrollability of events.

13. Finally, stop seeking hope in the eyes and words of people in power. Hope is for us to offer, not request. Whatever we seek from our leaders can ultimately only be found in the mirror. And that is not so bad.

Engaging Conversations

When engaging the help of others in getting something done, it helps to remember to go through the questions below in the three phases described. This allows you as the leader to make sure you are clear on the questions where there is less flexibility and discussion (*What and Why*) AND open to areas where there is room for others to experiment (*How*). The far right of the diagram shows the kind of language a leader might use when discussing a project/task with a team.

	Main Question	*Leader/ Teams Actions*	*What it sounds like*
①	**What?** **Why?**	**Leader offers/ clarifies**	"Here's what I think we need to do" or "What's your understanding of what we're trying to do?" "Let's talk about why this is important to the business, our department, the team, etc."
②	**Who?** **When?** **Where?**	**Leader & team define boundaries**	"Here's who needs to be involved…" "This is the timeline we're being asked to meet…" "This is where it will be implemented…" "This is our budget…"
③	**How?**	**Leader gets out of way; team *self-organizes***	"If you're clear on *what* we need to do and *why*, and the constraints we need to do it in, I'll leave the *how* to you. Let me know where I can help."